Monschau's Lucky 38th
Jason Boswell

Red Karnage Publishing—Colorado Springs, CO
ISBN: 978-0-578-78931-6
Library of Congress Control Number: 2020920990
Title: *Monschau's Lucky 38th*
Author: Jason Boswell
Digital distribution | 2020.
Paperback | 2020

Acknowledgements

I want to thank my wife, Kira, and children for being behind me in my studies and the entire process. Their work outside of my research proved indispensable and can never truly be repaid. My grandmother, Joanne Call, laid the foundation to this book. At a young age, she gave me her father's letters from World War II to read. As I poured over them, I learned about this amazing battle at Monschau. Her love was my desire to learn everything I could about the events at Monschau. To my parents to taught me the drive and power of an education. I am forever grateful to Dr. John Broom, my historian mentor, for his expert advice and continued editing. The constant phone calls and emails of continued encouragement helped me through some of the dark days of research. All the librarians and assistants at the Ike Skelton Library proved invaluable in helping find the many sources needed to bring this story together.

Lastly thank you to Erica Hughes for helping me publish this work. Your expertise along the way will always be greatly appreciated.

Table of Contents

Chapter I: Setting the Stage

"Know the enemy and know yourself; in a hundred
battles you will never be in peril"
-Sun Tzu

In the heavily wooded hills of the Ardennes forest along the Belgium-German border lies the small picturesque town of Monschau. Six months after the Allied invasion at Normandy, the United States (US) Army and other Allied countries had Hitler reeling back into Germany, scrambling for a victory that would turn the tide of the war back into Germany's favor. By the fall of 1944, Hitler and his Generals desperately looked to regain the initiative and control of the war. In the early hours of December 16, 1944, Adolf Hitler launched Operation Watch Over the Rhine, later known as the Ardennes Offensive or The Battle of the Bulge. Through September and into October 1944, the Allies ferociously fought in the Battle of the Hurtgen Forest, eventually pushing the Germans out of the Ardennes region and into Germany. After the bloody Battle of the Hurtgen Forest, the US V Corps ordered the 38th Cavalry Squadron (Mechanized) to occupy and defend the town of Monschau, while the Allies were preparing to cross the Rhine River and ultimately for the final invasion of Nazi Germany. The fighting that occurred during the Ardennes Offensive was incredibly fierce and under some of the worst

1

conditions. Despite these challenges, the 38th Cavalry Squadron was able to defend the German town of Monschau, holding the vital railroads and road network, against the German *LXVII Corps*. The result of the Allied victory at Monschau proved to be the most northern part of the Allies lines not fall to Hitler's advancing German Army.

Many statistics suggest that the Germans should have easily overwhelmed the 38th Cavalry Squadron, quickly advancing to the Belgium town of Eupen and capture the US V Corps headquarters. The 38th Cavalry Squadron consisted of approximately 800 soldiers and were able to defeat the much larger German force of approximately 18,000 soldiers. The *LXVII Corps* was able to penetrate the 38th Cavalry's defensive line and dropped German paratroopers between the 38th Cavalry and the US V Corps Headquarters. The entire 38th Cavalry Squadron became surrounded. The German attack caused discord among the 38th Cavalry to the point that wounded soldiers at the Squadron aid station found themselves with a weapon placed around the Squadron headquarters with orders to defend at all costs. The 38th Cavalry was outnumbered approximately 23:1 during the three-day defense and came out victorious, leading to the German Army's first defeat of the Ardennes Offensive. During the Ardennes Offensive, why did the Allies' "northern shoulder" hold its position in Monschau and not fall to the German *LXVII Corps*?

The 38th Cavalry Squadron attempted to abide by US Army doctrine in 1944. US Army Field Manual 100-5 gave specific guidance on cavalry units and defensive operations. For defensive operations, the field manual suggests that long gentle slopes were better than abrupt elevations, such as the terrain surrounding Monschau. When building a defense, the most crucial factor to be considered with regards to the terrain was to have good artillery observation, fields of fire, and obstacles.[1] The manual continues that when in a defense, US commanders must conduct continuous patrols to observe the enemy disposition and enemy offensive preparations. Commanders were always to be prepared to meet an attack that favors the attacker.[2] An aggressive defense was preferred. It was seldom feasible to hold a defensive position through passive resistance.[3] When identifying a defensive battle position, each position should not exceed the range of small arms, and important locations along the defensive line were to be defended to the last man possible.[4] 1944 doctrine also stated that when in the defense, artillery was to concentrate their fires on critical locations and beyond the range of supporting weapons but required good observation and signal communication.[5] Engineers were to be employed to impede the advance of the enemy and not as combat units.[6] Tank

---

[1] War Department, "FM 100-5 1944 (OBSOLETE): Field Service Regulations: Operations." n.d. Ike Skelton Combined Arms Research Library (CARL),162

[2] War Department, "FM 100-5 1944 (OBSOLETE)," 161, 163

[3] War Department, "FM 100-5 1944 (OBSOLETE)," 178-179

[4] War Department, "FM 100-5 1944 (OBSOLETE)," 164; 181

[5] War Department, "FM 100-5 1944 (OBSOLETE)," 170

[6] War Department, "FM 100-5 1944 (OBSOLETE)," 174-175

destroyers were not designed or intended for defensive operations and never mentions suggested use of tank destroyers in a defense.[7]

In World War II, the 38th Cavalry Squadron had a unique organizational structure and equipment. The 38th Cavalry consisted of three reconnaissance troops, a headquarters troop, a service troop, and a medical troop, combining for a total of 770 men.[8] Each reconnaissance troop (A Troop, B Troop, and C Troop) was authorized 17 .30 caliber machine guns, 15 .50 caliber machine guns (not including the weapons mounted on vehicles), three 81mm mortars, and nine armored personnel vehicles. The headquarters troop had six .30 caliber machine guns, ten .50 caliber machine guns (not including the weapons mounted on vehicles), and 11 armored personnel vehicles. The service troop (E Troop) had 17 M3 Stuart light tanks, but only two dismounted .30 caliber machine guns and three dismounted .50 caliber machine guns.[9] The 38th Cavalry Squadron also had 115 different radios to communicate across the Squadron.[10] The 38th Cavalry Squadron had seen

---

[7] War Department, "FM 100-5 1944 (OBSOLETE)," 189-190

[8] "Orgn and Equipment of Mechanized Cav Units." n.d. Ike Skelton Combined Arms Research Library (CARL) Digital Library. Accessed January 19, 2020, Tab E; War Department, "FM 2-30 1943 (OBSOLETE): Cavalry Field Manual, Cavalry Mechanized Reconnaissance Squadron." n.d. Ike Skelton Combined Arms Research Library (CARL) Digital Library. Obsolete Military Manuals. December 16, 2010, 93

[9] War Department, "FM 2-30 1943 (OBSOLETE)," 95-102

[10] War Department, "FM 2-30 1943 (OBSOLETE)," 103-105

action shortly after D-Day and presumably entered Monschau not at 100% combat strength or every single vehicle, machine gun, mortar, and radio operational. During World War II armored vehicles were best utilized for defensive operations. Light tanks were better suited for offensive operations, and their 37mm main gun was an ineffective weapon system except against personnel.[11] Cavalry units could be assigned five different types of operations. Defensive operations accounted for 32.8% of all missions in World War II. Dismounted defensive operations accounted for 63.9% of all defensive operations.[12]

The 38th Cavalry Squadron occupied the Monschau area on October 1st, 1944, as part of the US V Corps defensive line in anticipation of attacking across the Roer River dams and continuing deeper into Germany.[13] The different Allied units across the northern shoulder near Monschau range from US General Courtney Hodges and the First Army headquarters in Liege, Belgium to tank destroyer and engineer platoons in support of the 38th Cavalry Squadron.[14] In Liege, Belgium, approximately 60 kilometers west of Monschau, was the US First Army headquarters. General Hodges and the US V Corps headquarters were in Eupen, Belgium, approximately

---

[11] "Orgn and Equipment of Mechanized Cav Units," Tab D

[12] "Orgn and Equipment of Mechanized Cav Units," Tab C

[13] LTC (R) Shehab, Alfred H. M., n.d. "Cavalry On The Shoulder: The 38th CRS and the Defense of Monschau." NJ Cavalry and Armor Association. Accessed January 19, 2020, 1

[14] Shehab, "Cavalry On The Shoulder," 4.

20 kilometers west of Monschau. Both the US First Army headquarters and the US V Corps headquarters were along the critical Monschau-Eupen Road. In Eupen, the US V Corps supply depot held all the different classes of supply for the entire Corps. [15] The 395th Infantry Regiment occupied Hofen, Germany, to the south of Monschau, becoming the adjacent southern unit to the 38th Cavalry.[16] The 38th Cavalry Squadron fell under the 102nd Cavalry Group. As the 38th Cavalry began to occupy Monschau, the 102nd Cavalry Squadron, also a part of the 102nd Cavalry Group, occupied areas north of the 38th Cavalry. The 102nd Cavalry Group had a small reserve element consisting of A Company, 47th Infantry Regiment, and a platoon of M4 Sherman tanks from A Company, 10th Armored Battalion.[17] In late 1944 the US V Corp was beginning to assemble

---

[15] MAJ Rousek, Charles E., n.d. "A Short History of the 38th Cavalry Reconnaissance Squadron (Mechanized)." NJ Cavalry and Armor Association. Accessed January 19, 2020, 11; CPL Leone, Raymond J., n.d. "In Front of the Front-Line: WWII stories written by a Scout from the 38th Cavalry Reconnaissance Squadron Mechanized." NJ Cavalry and Armor Association. Accessed January 19, 2020.
http://njcavalryandarmorassociation.org/history.html, 47

[16] LTC O'Brien, Robert E., "After Action Report, 38th Cavalry Reconnaissance Squadron (Mechanized), Aug 44 thru April 45." n.d. Ike Skelton Combined Arms Research Library (CARL) Digital Library. 2011. World War II Operational Documents. May 16, 2011, 40; MAJ Way, David W., "Certificate," January 21, 1945. in "After Action Report, 38th Cavalry Reconnaissance Squadron (Mechanized), Aug 44 thru April 45." n.d. Ike Skelton Combined Arms Research Library (CARL) Digital Library. 2011. World War II Operational Documents. May 16, 2011, 1

[17] Shehab, "Cavalry On The Shoulder," 7

various combat units for a major attack to seize the Roer River dams that was scheduled to begin on December 14th. The 78th Infantry Division initiated the offensive and attacked Kesternich, Germany. [18] As the US V Corps moved different combat units in support of the attack to take control of the Roer River dams, the only combat unit left to defend the Monschau-Eupen Road was the 38th Cavalry Squadron.[19]

Monschau Germany lies less than five kilometers east of the Belgium border. As the 38th Cavalry began to occupy Monschau, its citizens displayed some anxiety toward Allied occupation.[20] The majority of Monschau itself was empty of civilians, but a large number of the local population remained.[21] The Germans were located less than three kilometers east of Monschau in Imgenbroich, German, and conducted harassing artillery fire in an attempt to disrupt the 38th Cavalry's occupation. To gain support from the local population, the Squadron aid station provided medical care to any civilian that was

---

[18] Shehab, "Cavalry On The Shoulder," 1; Rousek, "A Short History of the 38th Cavalry Reconnaissance Squadron (Mechanized)," 11

[19] Shehab, "Cavalry On The Shoulder," 4

[20] CPT Goetcheus, Robert A., "Military Government Periodic Report No. 78" in "After Action Report, 38th Cavalry Reconnaissance Squadron (Mechanized), Aug 44 thru April 45." n.d. Ike Skelton Combined Arms Research Library (CARL) Digital Library. 2011. World War II Operational Documents. May 16, 2011.

[21] Shehab, "Cavalry On The Shoulder," 4

affected by German artillery fire and attacks.[22] The 38th Cavalry's area of responsibility was so large that Colonel (COL) Robert E. O'Brien,[23] commander of the 38th Cavalry Squadron, could not afford to have a reserve force.[24] He placed the 38th Cavalry's main defensive line in the woods just to the east of Monschau proper overlooking open fields with hedgerows.[25]

In December 1944, COL O'Brien had all his organic elements along with a company of combat engineers and two platoons of M10 Tank Destroyers'. COL O'Brien arrayed his forces along a generally north to south running axis with his reconnaissance troops comprising the bulk of his defensive line. A Troop occupied the Konzen Railroad station five and a half kilometers north of Monschau.[26] 1st Platoon, A Troop was the northernmost 38th Cavalry element and

---

[22] O'Brien, "After Action Report, 38th Cavalry Reconnaissance Squadron (Mechanized), Aug 44 thru April 45," 44

[23] At the time of the Ardennes Offensive, Robert O'Brien was a Lieutenant Colonel.

[24] LTC (R) Shehab, Alfred H. M., "Defense of Monschau by the 38th Cavalry Squadron." August 29, 2019. 1; Rousek, "A Short History of the 38th Cavalry Reconnaissance Squadron (Mechanized)," 10

[25] O'Brien, "After Action Report, 38th Cavalry Reconnaissance Squadron (Mechanized), Aug 44 thru April 45," 40

[26] Leone, "In Front of the Front-Line," 40; LTC O'Brien, Robert E., "Operations Map #2," in "After Action Report, 38th Cavalry Reconnaissance Squadron (Mechanized), Aug 44 thru April 45." n.d. Ike Skelton Combined Arms Research Library (CARL) Digital Library. 2011. World War II Operational Documents. May 16, 2011.

stayed in contact with B Troop, 102nd Cavalry Squadron. To the south of 1st Platoon, was 3rd Platoon in the middle of A Troop defensive line, with 2nd Platoon being the southern limit of the A Troop line next to B Troop.[27] The distance between A Troop and B Troop was more than one and a half kilometers. This gap was visible to Germans in Imgenbroich and its surrounding ridge.[28] B Troop was committed to a three-kilometer front with 3rd Platoon next to A Troop in the north, 1st Platoon in the center, and 2nd Platoon in the south.[29] To the south of B Troop were tank destroyers from 1st Platoon, F Company. C Troop occupied a line of trenches on a hill east of Monschau with 3rd Platoon in the north tying in with 1st Platoon, F Company. 2nd Platoon was in the center, and 1st Platoon was in the south next to 2nd Platoon, F Company, the second platoon of tank destroyers. Also positioned on the outskirts of Eupen were Headquarters Troop and Service Troop command posts.[30]

---

[27] O'Brien, "After Action Report, 38th Cavalry Reconnaissance Squadron (Mechanized), Aug 44 thru April 45," 40; O'Brien, "Operations Map #2."

[28] Leone, "In Front of the Front-Line," 42; O'Brien, "Operations Map #2."

[29] CPT Sain, Joseph R., "Report of Captain Joseph R. Sain 0-1030828, Troop Commander, Troop B, 38th CAV RCN SQ," December 16-18, 1944. in "After Action Report, 38th Cavalry Reconnaissance Squadron (Mechanized), Aug 44 thru April 45." n.d. Ike Skelton Combined Arms Research Library (CARL) Digital Library. 2011. World War II Operational Documents. May 16, 2011, 1; O'Brien, "Operations Map #2."

[30] O'Brien, "After Action Report, 38th Cavalry Reconnaissance Squadron (Mechanized), Aug 44 thru April 45," 41; O'Brien, "Operations Map #2."

The German *LXVII Corps* that opposed the 38th Cavalry was structured to best support Hitler's operational plan for the Ardennes Offensive. The *LXVII Corps* was part of the *6th Panzer Army*. The *6th Panzer Army* had the *1st* and *2nd SS Panzer Corps* and the *LXVII Corps*.[31] The *6th Panzer Army* totaled four *Panzer Divisions*, to include the famous *1st SS Panzer Division*, at the disposal of *SS-Oberst-Gruppenfuhrer Josef Dietrich*[32], commander of the *6th Panzer Army*.[33] At the beginning of the Ardennes Offensive, the *LXVII Corps* had two Divisions. A third and fourth division, the *3rd Panzergrenadier Division* and the *246th Volksgrenadier Division*, was reassigned to the *LXVII Corps* on December 19th and 28th, 1944, respectively.[34] The *LXVII Corps* had been formed as a reserve in 1942 and transferred to the German *6th Panzer Army* for the Ardennes Offensive. The two divisions assigned to the *LXVII Corps* at the start of the Ardennes Offensive were the understrength *272nd* and *326th Volksgrenadier Divisions* with a combined

---

[31] Quarrie, Bruce, *The Ardennes Offensive: VI Panzer Armee: Northern Sector,* (Oxford: Osprey, 1999).21

[32] SS-Oberst-Gruppenfuhrer is translated to Colonel Group Leader. It is the highest rank that could be held in the German SS, next to Reichsfuhrer, which was held by Heinrich Himmler.

[33] Quarrie, *The Ardennes Offensive: VI Panzer Armee: Northern Sector,* 20; 1LT Ross, Wesley, "The Bulge: Per the 146th Engineer Combat Bn." February 3, 2014. http://battleofthebulgememories.be/stories26/us-army25/831-the-bulge-per-the-146th-engineer-combat-bn.html. 2-3

[34] Quarrie, *The Ardennes Offensive: VI Panzer Armee: Northern Sector,* 83, 85

strength of 17,854 soldiers.[35] Each division contained three infantry regiments, an additional infantry battalion, an artillery regiment, an antitank battalion, an antiaircraft battalion, an engineer battalion, a signal battalion, a supply company, a medical company, an administrative company, and a maintenance company.[36] *General der Infanterie Otto Hitzfeld* directed that the *272nd Volksgrenadier Division* stop the US 78th Infantry Divisions attack in Kesternich. The 326th Volksgrenadier Division was to attack Monschau. The *326th Volksgrenadier Division* had loaned an infantry battalion to the *272nd Volksgrenadier Division* in support of their defense.[37]

The three infantry regiments the belonged to the *326th Volksgrenadier Division* was the *751st, 752nd, and 753rd Regiments*. Each regiment was authorized three battalions consisting of three rifle company's, a staff company, and a support company. Each rifle company was to have nine light machine guns. The battalions support company required one heavy machine gun, eight light machine guns, six 80mm mortars, and four 75mm wheeled support guns. Each regiment's 2nd and 3rd Battalions was to have an additional artillery company that had four 120mm mortars, four 75mm wheeled support guns, and five light machine guns. 2nd and 3rd Battalions were also

[35] Dupuy, Trevor N., David L. Bongard, and Richard C. Anderson, *Hitler's Last Gamble: The Battle of the Bulge, December 1944-January 1945*, (New York: Harper Perennial, 1995) 476

[36] Quarrie, *The Ardennes Offensive: VI Panzer Armee: Northern Sector,* 81-82

[37] Quarrie, *The Ardennes Offensive: VI Panzer Armee: Northern Sector,* 82

authorized one tank destroyer company with 54 panzerfausts and four light machine guns. This brought an authorized total of approximately 1,760 fighting soldiers to each regiment. The *326th Volksgrenadier Division's* artillery regiment had three artillery battalions. The 1st artillery battalion had three artillery batteries, with each battery consisting of six 75mm howitzers. The 2nd and 3rd artillery battalions had four artillery batteries, with each battery having six 105mm howitzers. The artillery regiment had a 4th battalion that consisted of two batteries, each with six 150mm howitzers. The *326th Volksgrenadier Division's* anti-tank battalion consisted of three companies. The 1st and 2nd Company each had 14 75mm tracked assault guns, the Sturmgeschutz III, or 14 75mm tank destroyer, the Jagdpanzer. The 3rd Company consisted of 12 75mm anti-aircraft guns. The *326th Volksgrenadier Division* dedicated anti-aircraft battalion had three companies. The 1st and 2nd Company had four 88mm anti-aircraft guns. 3rd Company had six lighter 20mm anti-aircraft guns. Lastly, the *326th Volksgrenadier Division* Engineer Battalion had three companies. Each company consisted of two heavy machine guns, nine light machine guns, two 80mm mortars, and six flamethrowers. The *326th Volksgrenadier Division* was authorized a total of nine heavy machine guns, 144 light machine guns, 90 75mm guns (either wheeled or tracked), 110 artillery pieces (mortar and howitzer), 26 anti-aircraft guns, and various other small arms. The total authorized size of the *326th Volksgrenadier Division* was between 10,000 to

12,000 men.[38]   At the beginning of the Ardennes Offensive, the *326th Volksgrenadier Division* had roughly 9,000 men, nine towed anti-tank weapons, 79 light artillery guns, and 18 medium artillery pieces.[39] The *326th Volksgrenadier Division* was understaffed and underequipped at the start of the Ardennes Offensive but maintained enough combat power to overwhelm the 38th Cavalry Squadron.

General der Infanterie Otto Hitzfeld knew that the weakened *326th Volksgrenadier Division* would need additional support if it was going to be successful in securing Monschau.   The *326th Volksgrenadier Division* had two Artillery Corps and two Nebelwerfer Rocket Brigades in support.   Each artillery Corps consisted of five battalions, resulting in over 120 artillery guns in direct support of the *326th Volksgrenadier Division*.[40]   The *326th Volksgrenadier Division's* three infantry regiments were all located in the vicinity of Imgenbroich. The *751st Regiment* was to the west of Imgenbroich in pillboxes and trenches. The *752nd Regiment* was to the south of Imgenbroich, and the *753rd Regiment* became the Division reserve.   The *326th Volksgrenadier Division* placed eight 75mm guns and mortars in the low ground on the east side of Imgenbroich.[41]   To prepare for the Ardennes

---

[38] Quarrie, *The Ardennes Offensive: VI Panzer Armee: Northern Sector,* 10-11

[39] Dupuy, *Hitler's Last Gamble: The Battle of the Bulge, December 1944-January 1945,* 476, 480

[40] Shehab, "Cavalry On The Shoulder," 4

[41] CPT Frink, George R., "S-2 Estimate of Enemy Forces to Immediate Front of 38th Cav on 17 December 1944, as result of PW Interrogation," January 11, 1945. in "After Action

Offensive, the *326ᵗʰ Volksgrenadier Division* kept most of its combat power in Schleiden, Germany, approximately 28 kilometers east of Imgenbroich. The soldiers of the *326ᵗʰ Volksgrenadier Division* marched throughout the night of December 15-16, arriving mere hours before the attack.[42] Regardless of the all-night march, German morale was high on the morning of December 16ᵗʰ.[43]

The German *6ᵗʰ Panzer Army* plan was to reach the Baraque Michel crossroads, midway between Malmedy and Eupen, by the night of December 16ᵗʰ. The *6ᵗʰ Panzer Army's 3ʳᵈ Fallschirmjager (Airborne) Division*s objective was to secure these crossroads.[44] With the *272ⁿᵈ Volksgrenadier Division* actively fighting the US 78ᵗʰ Infantry Division, the *326ᵗʰ Volksgrenadier Division*s objective was relatively simple. The *751ˢᵗ Regiment*

Report, 38th Cavalry Reconnaissance Squadron (Mechanized), Aug 44 thru April 45." n.d. Ike Skelton Combined Arms Research Library (CARL) Digital Library. 2011. World War II Operational Documents. May 16, 2011.

[42] 1LT O'Brien, James J., "Report of 1st LT James J. O'Brien, Platoon Leader, 1st Platoon, Tr C," in "After Action Report, 38th Cavalry Reconnaissance Squadron (Mechanized), Aug 44 thru April 45." n.d. Ike Skelton Combined Arms Research Library (CARL) Digital Library. 2011. World War II Operational Documents. May 16, 2011, 1

[43] 2LT Harf, Arthur, "Consolidated Interrogated Report of P/W's captured 16-18 Dec 44," January 25, 1945. in "After Action Report, 38th Cavalry Reconnaissance Squadron (Mechanized), Aug 44 thru April 45." n.d. Ike Skelton Combined Arms Research Library (CARL) Digital Library. 2011. World War II Operational Documents. May 16, 2011.

[44] Ross, "The Bulge: Per the 146th Engineer Combat Bn.," 3

was to take the Hofen, Germany, along a railroad west of the Monschau-Eupen Road. The *752nd Regiment* was to capture Roehren and take the high ground between Monschau and Hofen.[45] The plan of securing both the *751st* and *752nd Regiment's* objectives would allow the *326th Volksgrenadier Division* to capture Monschau. The *2nd SS Panzer Division* and the *Grossdeutschland Brigade* would then relieve the *326th Volksgrenadier Division.*[46]

The 38th Cavalry Squadron had been in constant combat for nearly two months when they arrived in Monschau. The moral of the 38th Cavalry was generally high. The Monschau area had an abundance of deer and boars, and the 38th Cavalry took opportunities to enjoy venison every few days.[47] Soldiers even had opportunities to enjoy movies at the Monschau theater.[48] However, the weather began to turn cold and wet at the beginning of November, and much-needed winter clothing did not arrive until late November.[49] Throughout the occupation of Monschau, the 38th Cavalry soldiers occupied empty houses when not on patrol or in defensive positions in

---

[45] Harf, "Consolidated Interrogated Report of P/W's captured 16-18 Dec 44."; Frink, "S-2 Estimate of Enemy Forces to Immediate Front of 38th Cav on 17 December 1944, as result of PW Interrogation."

[46] Harf, "Consolidated Interrogated Report of P/W's captured 16-18 Dec 44."

[47] Tec. 4 Russell Taylor to Mary Taylor, 2 November 1944, private collection

[48] Tec. 4 Russell Taylor to Mary Taylor, 19 November 1944, private collection

[49] Tec. 4 Russell Taylor to Mary Taylor, 7 & 21 November 1944, private collection

an attempt to stay warm and out of the deteriorating weather conditions.[50]

On December 1st, 1944, all 38th Cavalry defensive positions were in place.[51] 2nd and 3rd Battalions of the 60th Infantry Regiment moved into positions behind A and B Troop and began digging a secondary defensive line. Six days later, on December 6th, the 60th Infantry Regiment was replaced by the 2nd Battalion, 16th Infantry Regiment.[52] During the second week of December, the 38th Cavalry started receiving information that a German Armored Division had moved into Imgenbroich.[53] In an attempt to continue the pressure of the US V Corps attack to secure the Roer River dams, the 2nd Battalion, 16th Infantry, was ordered to leave the Monschau area on December 15th.[54] Demolition was placed on all the bridges around Monschau as combat units began to evacuate the area. The local population became apprehensive, but members of the 38th Cavalry helped calm their worries. Any attempt to conduct mass civilian evacuations would not have been possible.[55]

---

[50] Tec. 4 Russell Taylor to Mary Taylor, 21 November 1944, private collection

[51] O'Brien, "After Action Report, 38th Cavalry Reconnaissance Squadron (Mechanized), Aug 44 thru April 45," 41

[52] O'Brien, "After Action Report, 38th Cavalry Reconnaissance Squadron (Mechanized), Aug 44 thru April 45," 40-42

[53] Leone, "In Front of the Front-Line," 45

[54] O'Brien, "After Action Report, 38th Cavalry Reconnaissance Squadron (Mechanized), Aug 44 thru April 45," 42

[55] Goetcheus, "Military Government Periodic Report No. 78"

The 38th Cavalry not only had to fight the Germans but also had to contend with the local population in Monschau, adding another element of complexity to the battlefield.   A German messenger from *1st Battalion, 752nd Regiment, 326th Volksgrenadier Division*, had gotten lost on December 15th and was taken prisoner in Kesternich.   During his interrogation, he stated that the *326th Volksgrenadier Division* had reorganized in Hungary and went to Trier, German, three weeks prior. Since their arrival in Trier, the division had been slowly marching the 115 kilometers to Imgenbroich.[56]

[56] Harf, "Consolidated Interrogated Report of P/W's captured 16-18 Dec 44."

Chapter II: The Attack

"In every battle there comes a time when both sides consider themselves beaten, then he who continues the attack wins."
-General Ulysses S. Grant

T he morning of December, 16th was cold and snowing.[57] At 5:30 am, German artillery and rocket fire hit the 38th Cavalry defensive line, concentrating on the Squadron command post and C Troop, and continued west into the Allied artillery positions.[58] The Squadron command post and aid station received approximately 200 rounds of artillery in the 25 minutes that German artillery fell along the 38th Cavalry defensive line.[59] North of the 38th Cavalry command post, B Troop, received approximately 1,000 rounds of artillery throughout the day.[60] At 6:00 am, German planes began

---

[57] Leone, "In Front of the Front-Line," 46

[58] Rousek, "A Short History of the 38th Cavalry Reconnaissance Squadron (Mechanized)," 11; O'Brien, "After Action Report, 38th Cavalry Reconnaissance Squadron (Mechanized), Aug 44 thru April 45," 44

[59] O'Brien, "After Action Report, 38th Cavalry Reconnaissance Squadron (Mechanized), Aug 44 thru April 45," 44

[60] Sain, "Report of Captain Joseph R. Sain 0-1030828, Troop Commander, Troop B, 38th CAV RCN SQ," 1

dropping flares lighting up the entire C Troop area.[61] The *326th Volksgrenadier Division* conducted a Battalion frontal attack with all Battalion and Regiment supporting weapons in direct support.[62] At 6:05 am *3rd Company, 1st Battalion, 751st Regiment* initiated the attack on Monschau.[63] At this same time, 2nd Platoon F Company began hearing movement on Menzerath Hill, a predominant terrain feature between Monschau and Imgenbroich, and received small arms fire.[64] The Squadron command post received a report from A Troop at 6:15 am that to the north, the 78th Infantry Division was under

---

[61] 1LT Coleman, Raphail V., "Report of 1st LT Raphail V. Coleman, Platoon Leader, 3rd Platoon, Troop C, 38 Cav. Rcn. Sq.," December 16-17, 1944. in "After Action Report, 38th Cavalry Reconnaissance Squadron (Mechanized), Aug 44 thru April 45." n.d. Ike Skelton Combined Arms Research Library (CARL) Digital Library. 2011. World War II Operational Documents. May 16, 2011, 1

[62] CPT Frink, George R., Report Title Unreadable, in "After Action Report, 38th Cavalry Reconnaissance Squadron (Mechanized), Aug 44 thru April 45." n.d. Ike Skelton Combined Arms Research Library (CARL) Digital Library. 2011. World War II Operational Documents. May 16, 2011.

[63] O'Brien, "After Action Report, 38th Cavalry Reconnaissance Squadron (Mechanized), Aug 44 thru April 45," 45; Shehab, "Cavalry On The Shoulder," 5

[64] O'Brien, "After Action Report, 38th Cavalry Reconnaissance Squadron (Mechanized), Aug 44 thru April 45," 44; S/SGT Bielicki, Bernard C., "Report of Staff Sergeant Bernard C. Bielicki, Platoon Sergeant, 2nd Platoon, Company F, 38th CAV RCN SQ (MECZ)," December 16, 1944. in "After Action Report, 38th Cavalry Reconnaissance Squadron (Mechanized), Aug 44 thru April 45." n.d. Ike Skelton Combined Arms Research Library (CARL) Digital Library. 2011. World War II Operational Documents. May 16, 2011.

attack in Kesternich.[65]   As the battle continued, German snipers began to focus their efforts in the area of 2nd Platoon, F Company inflicting casualties. 2nd Platoon, F Company's wounded would not be sent to the Squadron air station until 9:30 am. A little over an hour later, members of 2nd Platoon, F Company, were able to identify and destroy the German sniper position with small arms fire. With the German sniper killed, sniper fire in the 2nd Platoons area became less frequent.[66] As the afternoon approached, the C Troop command post received accurate German mortar, artillery, and rocket fire.[67]   Greatly outnumbered, the 38th Cavalry began to understand the situation and that a major German offensive was underway. They requested reinforcements from the 102nd Cavalry Group at 12:40 pm.[68] Two and a half hours later, more accurate German mortar, artillery, and rockets again attack the C Troop command

---

[65] O'Brien, "After Action Report, 38th Cavalry Reconnaissance Squadron (Mechanized), Aug 44 thru April 45," 45

[66] Bielicki, "Report of Staff Sergeant Bernard C. Bielicki, Platoon Sergeant, 2nd Platoon, Company F, 38th CAV RCN SQ (MECZ)."

[67] CPT Rogers, Elmer L., "Report of Capitan Elmer L. Rogers, Commanding Officer, Troop C, 38th CAV RCN SQ (MECZ)," in "After Action Report, 38th Cavalry Reconnaissance Squadron (Mechanized), Aug 44 thru April 45." n.d. Ike Skelton Combined Arms Research Library (CARL) Digital Library. 2011. World War II Operational Documents. May 16, 2011.

[68] O'Brien, "After Action Report, 38th Cavalry Reconnaissance Squadron (Mechanized), Aug 44 thru April 45," 46

post.[69]

At 3:25 pm, small elements behind the 38th Cavalry began to understand the dire situation they would find themselves in, and the consequences if the Germans broke through the 38th Cavalry defensive lines. The commander of the 1121st Combat Engineer Group deployed B Company with orders to form a defensive line between Monschau and Elsenborn to slow the German *6th Panzer Army*. B Company's main form of defense was a network of antitank mines that would create a series of roadblocks. B Company had also expertly placed explosives on trees in such a way that would allow the trees to fall into an abatis along the roads. B Company emplaced three machine-gun positions. One position had a .30 caliber machine gun, another had a .50 caliber machine gun, and the last position contained a water-cooled World War I era .30 caliber machine gun. During the night of December 16th, this .30 caliber machine gun would prove ineffective as the water froze, making the machine gun inoperable.[70]

COL O'Brien understood the importance of having a reserve element. As night approached, he designated the attached engineer company, A Company, 146th Engineer Battalion, as the Squadron reserve. At 5 pm, B and C Troop received 1st and 2nd Platoon of A Company to bolster their defensive line. 3rd Platoon, A Company was dug in to protect the

---

[69] Rogers, "Report of Capitan Elmer L. Rogers, Commanding Officer, Troop C, 38th CAV RCN SQ (MECZ)."

[70] Ross, "The Bulge: Per the 146th Engineer Combat Bn.," 3

southern flank of the Squadron headquarters.[71] A Squadron alternate command post was established near the C Troop mortars in anticipation of the Squadron command post becoming attacked or hit by German artillery. C Troop positions continued to receive German artillery and rocket attacks throughout the night.[72] During the night, the Germans utilized five big searchlights to bounce light off the low lying clouds to put artificial light on Menzerath Hill and the 38th Cavalry's defensive positions.[73] As reports of German attacks across the Allied front spread, every command post in the rear area of the 38th Cavalry heightened security and placed armored vehicles at key intersections in anticipation of a German breakthrough of the 38th Cavalry defensive lines. The Squadron Intelligence Officer, Capitan George Frink, summarized that the German attacks and patrols of December 16th were the German attempt to recon the 38th Cavalry positions in preparation for a larger attack.[74] Similar to CPT Frink's assessment, echelons above the 38th Cavalry recognized that the 38th Cavalry was largely outnumbered against the German *LXVII Corps* and began to consider their options in stopping the German Ardennes Offensive.

---

[71] Rousek, "A Short History of the 38th Cavalry Reconnaissance Squadron (Mechanized)," 12

[72] O'Brien, "Report of 1st LT James J. O'Brien, Platoon Leader, 1st Platoon, Tr C," 1

[73] Rousek, "A Short History of the 38th Cavalry Reconnaissance Squadron (Mechanized)," 12

[74] O'Brien, "After Action Report, 38th Cavalry Reconnaissance Squadron (Mechanized), Aug 44 thru April 45," 46

The 38th Cavalry continued to maintain all machine gun positions and control the Monschau-Eupen Road during the night from December 16th to December 17th. At 1:30 am on December 17th, elements of the German *3rd Fallschirmjager (Airborne) Division* began to fall from the sky.[75] *General Friedrich August Freiherr von der Heydte*[76] was in charge of the German paratroopers who fell behind the 38th Cavalry Squadron's lines.[77] *General von der Heydte* and his paratroopers were no strangers to the 38th Cavalry as they had encountered each other in the hedgerows at Normandy.[78] The Ardennes Offensive's original airborne operation was scheduled to occur on

---

[75] Quarrie, *The Ardennes Offensive: VI Panzer Armee: Northern Sector,* 36; Leone, "In Front of the Front-Line," 46; Frink, Report Title Unreadable; 2LT Shehab, Alfred H.M., "Extract of Statement of LT. Alfred H.M. Shehab in Recommendation of Award for Sergeant Florantius Becker," in "After Action Report, 38th Cavalry Reconnaissance Squadron (Mechanized), Aug 44 thru April 45." n.d. Ike Skelton Combined Arms Research Library (CARL) Digital Library. 2011. World War II Operational Documents. May 16, 2011.

[76] At the time of the Ardennes Offensive, Friedrich August Freiherr von der Heydte held the rank of Colonel-Lt. Colonel-Lt is translated to Lieutenant Colonel. After World War II, Friedrich August Freiherr von der Heydte continued his military service in the armed forces of West Germany, where he achieved the rank of General.

[77] Colonel-Lt. Freiherr Von Der Heydte to The Commanding Officer of the Military Government at Monschau, December 22, 1944, in "After Action Report, 38th Cavalry Reconnaissance Squadron (Mechanized), Aug 44 thru April 45." n.d. Ike Skelton Combined Arms Research Library (CARL) Digital Library. 2011. World War II Operational Documents. May 16, 2011.

[78] Leone, "In Front of the Front-Line," 47

the night of December 15th. However, it was delayed due to logistical issues of obtaining fuel and getting the paratroopers assembled in the correct location.[79] The force of 1,500 soldiers fell from a height of 500 feet above the ground.[80] The paratroopers were scatted over 25 miles, from Eupen to Malmedy, due to high winds, inexperienced pilots, and no time to plan before the airborne operation properly.[81] The paratroopers hastily planned to rally together at a location that also happened to be a 1121st Engineer Battalion command post.[82] This complicated *General von der Heydte's* mission as his paratroopers were unable to find each other or other Germans.[83]

As the German paratroopers fell, 3rd Platoon, B Troop fired .50 caliber machine guns at the German paratroopers.[84] By 6 am, the Squadron was fully alert and had every Soldier in position to defend against

---

[79] Ross, "The Bulge: Per the 146th Engineer Combat Bn.," 2

[80] Ross, "The Bulge: Per the 146th Engineer Combat Bn.," 2; Frink, Report Title Unreadable; S/SGT Lindquist, Kenneth C., "Affidavit," January 18, 1945. in "After Action Report, 38th Cavalry Reconnaissance Squadron (Mechanized), Aug 44 thru April 45." n.d. Ike Skelton Combined Arms Research Library (CARL) Digital Library. 2011. World War II Operational Documents. May 16, 2011.

[81] Ross, "The Bulge: Per the 146th Engineer Combat Bn.," 2

[82] Ross, "The Bulge: Per the 146th Engineer Combat Bn.," 5

[83] Colonel-Lt. Freiherr Von Der Heydte to The Commanding Officer of the Military Government at Monschau, December 22, 1944.

[84] Shehab, "Defense of Monschau by the 38th Cavalry Squadron," 1

another German attack.[85] Elements of the 38th Cavalry did not have to wait long, and by 6:15 am, C Troop mortars and the Squadron alternate command post received German artillery fire.[86] 1st Platoon, F Company began to hear movement in the obstacles they had placed in the front of their positions. They fired small arms and .30 caliber machine guns and repelled the small German attack.[87] The German's attempted to infiltrate the 38th Cavalry's defensive line between 2nd Platoon, B Troop, and 3rd Platoon F Company.[88] To draw attention away from the leading German attack, the *752nd Regiment* conducted another frontal attack down the "Snake Road,"[89] lasting from 6:50 am to 8:00 am.[90] C Troop and F Company become engaged in an intense small arms firefight.[91]

---

[85] 2LT Ketz, Howard E., "Report of 2nd LT Ketz, Platoon Leader, 1st Platoon, Company F," December 17, 1944. in "After Action Report, 38th Cavalry Reconnaissance Squadron (Mechanized), Aug 44 thru April 45." n.d. Ike Skelton Combined Arms Research Library (CARL) Digital Library. 2011. World War II Operational Documents. May 16, 2011, 1

[86] Rousek, "A Short History of the 38th Cavalry Reconnaissance Squadron (Mechanized)," 12; O'Brien, "After Action Report, 38th Cavalry Reconnaissance Squadron (Mechanized), Aug 44 thru April 45," 47

[87] Ketz, "Report of 2nd LT Ketz, Platoon Leader, 1st Platoon, Company F," 1

[88] CPL Brown, Walter E., "Affidavit," January 24, 1945. in "After Action Report, 38th Cavalry Reconnaissance Squadron (Mechanized), Aug 44 thru April 45." n.d. Ike Skelton Combined Arms Research Library (CARL) Digital Library. 2011. World War II Operational Documents. May 16, 2011.

[89] This location is described in detail on page 35

[90] Frink, Report Title Unreadable

[91] 2LT Yontz, W. J., "Report of 1st LT. W. J. Yontz, Platoon Leader, 2nd Platoon, Troop B, Action of 17 December

At 7 am, the first wave of the leading German assault began their movement from Imgenbroich.[92] Lead elements of this wave, reached 3rd Platoon, F Company with German mortar support. 3rd Platoon, F Company repelled this attack with small arms fire, forcing the Germans into two groups. One group moved toward the "hairpin turn"[93] and the second group began moving north toward B Troop.[94] As the *752nd Regiment* attacks on C Troop began to come to a halt, the German paratroopers became active in the areas surrounding 1st Platoon, B Troop, and A Troop.[95] The German objective for December 17th

---

1944," in "After Action Report, 38th Cavalry Reconnaissance Squadron (Mechanized), Aug 44 thru April 45." n.d. Ike Skelton Combined Arms Research Library (CARL) Digital Library. 2011. World War II Operational Documents. May 16, 2011, 1

[92] O'Brien, "After Action Report, 38th Cavalry Reconnaissance Squadron (Mechanized), Aug 44 thru April 45," 47

[93] This location is described on page 35

[94] 1LT Cullinan, Robert J., "Report of 1st LT. Robert J. Cullinan 1032424 Platoon Leader, 3rd Platoon, Company F, 38th CAV RCN SQ," in "After Action Report, 38th Cavalry Reconnaissance Squadron (Mechanized), Aug 44 thru April 45." n.d. Ike Skelton Combined Arms Research Library (CARL) Digital Library. 2011. World War II Operational Documents. May 16, 2011, 1; TEC/5 Gier, Joseph C., "Report of Joseph C. Gier 32583371, 3rd Platoon, Company F, 38th CAV RCN SQ (MECZ)," December 17, 1944. in "After Action Report, 38th Cavalry Reconnaissance Squadron (Mechanized), Aug 44 thru April 45." n.d. Ike Skelton Combined Arms Research Library (CARL) Digital Library. 2011. World War II Operational Documents. May 16, 2011.

[95] Frink, Report Title Unreadable; Shehab, "Extract of Statement of LT. Alfred H.M. Shehab in Recommendation of Award for Sergeant Florantius Becker."

was to find a weak point in the B Troop defensive lines. The Germans had the advantage of superior numbers and using the hedgerows to cover their movement as they approached B Troop.[96] At 8:45 am seven Germans surrendered to 1st Platoon, F Company.[97] During interrogation, one of the German prisoners of war stated that the main German attack had yet to occur.[98] The second wave of German infantry began to assault B Troop positions around 9 am from Menzerath Hill. With the amount of German infantry assaulting the B Troop positions, the Squadron reserve engineer platoon was sent to reinforce B Troop.

The situation looked dire for the 38th Cavalry around 10 am and, over the next hour, they were on the brink of defeat. The 17th, 62nd, and 955th Field Artillery Battalions, artillery units that fired in support of the 38th Cavalry's defense, were positioned behind the main defensive line with forward observers near and on the main line of defense for the 38th Cavalry. Shortly before 10 am, all the field artillery units supporting the 38th Cavalry reported that German infantry was overrunning some of their observation posts, resulting in the field artillery observation posts having to destroy their equipment. The loss of field artillery forward observers significantly reduced the volume and accuracy of

[96] Yontz, "Report of 1st LT. W. J. Yontz, Platoon Leader, 2nd Platoon, Troop B, Action of 17 December 1944," 1

[97] Ketz, "Report of 2nd LT Ketz, Platoon Leader, 1st Platoon, Company F," 1

[98] Rousek, "A Short History of the 38th Cavalry Reconnaissance Squadron (Mechanized)," 13

Allied artillery fire. The advancing German infantry was able to place a machine gun position behind C Troop and 1st Platoon, F Company, on a high ridge overlooking Monschau. As C Troop continued to fight the remaining remnants of the morning attack along "snake road," they were attacked by German infantry to the north; all while being subjected to machine-gun fire from behind their positions.[99] The *326th Volksgrenadier Division* was beginning to impose its will on the 38th Cavalry Squadron. German infantry started to overrun B Troop and field artillery observation posts, and C Troop found themselves under attack from multiple directions.

The Squadron command post and the 102nd Cavalry Group discussed reinforcements as B Troop was still under attack. At 10:30 am, the B Troop Fire Support Officer saw the advancing German infantry to his immediate front and northern flank. German artillery fire directly hit his vehicle as he was attempting to direct artillery fire, forcing him to make his way to the B Troop command post.[100] At the same time, another B Troop observation post was attacked and overrun by German infantry. The US soldiers were cut off from B Troop and fled, making their way back to the 186th Field Artillery Battalion. The loss of these positions greatly hindered B Troop's

---

[99] O'Brien, "After Action Report, 38th Cavalry Reconnaissance Squadron (Mechanized), Aug 44 thru April 45," 47-50

[100] 1LT Comfort, James A., "Certificate," January 22, 1945. in "After Action Report, 38th Cavalry Reconnaissance Squadron (Mechanized), Aug 44 thru April 45." n.d. Ike Skelton Combined Arms Research Library (CARL) Digital Library. 2011. World War II Operational Documents. May 16, 2011, 2

primary means of support for calling in artillery fire.[101] Just before 11 am, two battalions from the *751ˢᵗ Regiment* infiltrated the B Troop defensive lines and began occupying positions, successfully penetrating the 38th Cavalry's defensive line.[102] More than 150 German infantry overran 2nd Platoon, B Troop's positions.[103] As the *751ˢᵗ Regiment* began to exploit the penetration of the Allied defensive lines, A Company, 47th Infantry Regiment, and a platoon of M4 Sherman tanks from 10th Tank Battalion, reinforcements sent from the 102nd Cavalry Group, arrived at the 38th Cavalry Squadron command post. The reinforcements were immediately sent towards B Troop to help stop the German penetration. As B Troop and the Squadron began to make a new defensive line and prepare for a counterattack, A Company, 47th Infantry, were ordered to patrol behind the new defensive line of B Troop, looking for

---

[101] PFC Pirera, Joseph B., "Affidavit," in "After Action Report, 38th Cavalry Reconnaissance Squadron (Mechanized), Aug 44 thru April 45." n.d. Ike Skelton Combined Arms Research Library (CARL) Digital Library. 2011. World War II Operational Documents. May 16, 2011.

[102] Frink, Report Title Unreadable; O'Brien, "After Action Report, 38th Cavalry Reconnaissance Squadron (Mechanized), Aug 44 thru April 45," 49

[103] PFC Riegel, Bernard F., "Affidavit," January 24, 1945. in "After Action Report, 38th Cavalry Reconnaissance Squadron (Mechanized), Aug 44 thru April 45." n.d. Ike Skelton Combined Arms Research Library (CARL) Digital Library. 2011. World War II Operational Documents. May 16, 2011; Sain, "Report of Captain Joseph R. Sain 0-1030828, Troop Commander, Troop B, 38th CAV RCN SQ," 2; Rousek, "A Short History of the 38th Cavalry Reconnaissance Squadron (Mechanized)," 14

pockets of the enemy.[104] The *326th Volksgrenadier Division* added another element to the battle. German Me-109 fighter planes began to make numerous strafing runs over the 38th Cavalry defensive positions. The Me-109 fighters flew over the Monschau area between 11:30 am and 2 pm.[105] At 11:45 am, as B Troop's 1st and 2nd Platoons were under siege, and their attached tank destroyers were having to fall back, 3rd Platoon received heavy German artillery fire and the B Troop command post engaged in small arms fire within 100 meters.[106] Shortly after the intense firefight at the B Troop command post, B Troop received the engineer reinforcements and two additional tank destroyers from F Company.[107] The tank destroyers and engineers, along with 2nd Platoon B Troop, lead the 38th Cavalry's counterattack by sweeping down the roads with the B Troop command post calling for artillery support.[108]

Around this time, A Troop sent information to the 38th Cavalry Squadron command post, that a prisoner

---

[104] O'Brien, "After Action Report, 38th Cavalry Reconnaissance Squadron (Mechanized), Aug 44 thru April 45," 50; Rousek, "A Short History of the 38th Cavalry Reconnaissance Squadron (Mechanized)," 13; Shehab, "Cavalry On The Shoulder," 7

[105] Shehab, "Cavalry On The Shoulder," 7; Cullinan, "Report of 1st LT. Robert J. Cullinan 1032424 Platoon Leader, 3rd Platoon, Company F, 38th CAV RCN SQ," 1

[106] Sain, "Report of Captain Joseph R. Sain 0-1030828, Troop Commander, Troop B, 38th CAV RCN SQ," 1-2

[107] Yontz, "Report of 1st LT. W. J. Yontz, Platoon Leader, 2nd Platoon, Troop B, Action of 17 December 1944," 1

[108] Rousek, "A Short History of the 38th Cavalry Reconnaissance Squadron (Mechanized)," 12

of war stated that a larger German attack was to be launched that afternoon. Rear-echelon maintenance, supply, and wounded personnel found themselves defending the Squadron command post as the intensity of the battle rose.[109] As the squadron command post mulled its options, the 102nd Cavalry Group sent word that the reinforcements requested the day prior were on their way.[110] The 38th Cavalry responded that they believed a larger German attack had yet to come. Understanding the desperate situation of the 38th Cavalry, the 102nd Cavalry Group radioed that the US 47th Infantry Regiment of the US 9th Infantry Division was sent to Monschau to reinforce the 38th Cavalry.[111]

After 90 minutes of close, intense fighting, B Troop began to occupy their original defensive positions. As 2nd Platoon, B Troop occupied their original positions, they immediately identified 75 German infantry moving west to reinforce the German penetration.[112] Artillery fire stopped the

---

[109] Rousek, "A Short History of the 38th Cavalry Reconnaissance Squadron (Mechanized)," 13-14; O'Brien, "After Action Report, 38th Cavalry Reconnaissance Squadron (Mechanized), Aug 44 thru April 45," 51

[110] The reinforcements the 102nd Cavalry Group referenced was A Company, 47th Infantry Regiment and the platoon of M4 Sherman tanks from the 10th Tank Battalion that had already arrived at the 38th Cavalry Squadron's command post.

[111] O'Brien, "After Action Report, 38th Cavalry Reconnaissance Squadron (Mechanized), Aug 44 thru April 45," 50-51

[112] Yontz, "Report of 1st LT. W. J. Yontz, Platoon Leader, 2nd Platoon, Troop B, Action of 17 December 1944," 1;

German reinforcements. During the B Troop counterattack, an estimated 50-60 German infantry snuck through 1st and 2nd Platoon, B Troop, who were presumably met by A Company, 47th Infantry. By 3:30 pm the B Troop original defensive lines were reinforced. Shortly before nightfall, B Troop received the reinforcement platoon of M4 Sherman tanks from the 10th Tank Battalion.[113] The M4 Sherman had become the 38th Cavalry Squadron's mobile reserve.[114] When ordered to reinforce the 38th Cavalry, the 47th Infantry Regiment was informed that the 38th Cavalry was utterly wiped out and destroyed.[115] With only this information and not fully understanding the situation near Monschau, the 47th Infantry Regiment moved slowly and cautiously toward Monschau. At 5 pm, the 47th Infantry was approximately five kilometers west of Monschau in Mutzenich.[116] An hour and a half later, the 47th Infantry arrived at the 38th Cavalry's command post in Monschau, stabilizing the defensive line. Ammunition and ration trucks continued to drive much-needed supplies throughout the day to the 38th

Sain, "Report of Captain Joseph R. Sain 0-1030828, Troop Commander, Troop B, 38th CAV RCN SQ," 2

[113] Yontz, "Report of 1st LT. W. J. Yontz, Platoon Leader, 2nd Platoon, Troop B, Action of 17 December 1944," 1-2

[114] Rousek, "A Short History of the 38th Cavalry Reconnaissance Squadron (Mechanized)," 13

[115] Shehab, "Defense of Monschau by the 38th Cavalry Squadron," 2

[116] Rousek, "A Short History of the 38th Cavalry Reconnaissance Squadron (Mechanized)," 13

Cavalry along the vital Monschau-Eupen Road.[117] During the confusion of the battle and the events occurring at the time, the A Troop's prisoner of war information regarding a larger German attack referenced the second wave of German infantry that had already attacked B Troop.

The Germans continued their use of pyrotechnics and searchlights through the night of December 17th into the early hours of December 18th. At 3:30 am, German planes dropped flares, and the entire Monschau and Hofen area received heavy German artillery and rocket attacks. An hour later, the *326th Volksgrenadier Division* began their main attack of the day south of Monschau on the 395th Infantry Regiment in Hofen, Germany. By 10:30 am, the German attack penetrated the 395th Infantry's defensive line with German tank support. At 11:10 am, word of German tanks supporting the German attack in Hofen reached the 38th Cavalry command post through the reports from the 406th Field Artillery Group. The German penetration in Hofen began to depict Monschau as the linchpin to holding the northern shoulder. At this time in the battle, the 38th Cavalry Squadron had Germans to their east and south. With the 395th Infantry Regiment unable to hold their positions in Hofen, the *326th Volksgrenadier Division* attempted to flank Monschau and the 38th Cavalry from Hofen Hill. The German infantry was once again able to achieve another penetration of the 38th Cavalry defensive

---

[117] O'Brien, "After Action Report, 38th Cavalry Reconnaissance Squadron (Mechanized), Aug 44 thru April 45," 51-52

lines.[118] This penetration was slow to develop as the Germans ensured they reinforced the positions they controlled before attempting to attack other positions. The fighting was deliberate as the 47th Infantry Regiment moved into supporting positions near C Troop and 3rd Platoon, F Company. Throughout the day, the 3,000 soldiers of the 47th Infantry Regiment began to relieve the 38th Cavalry Squadron, starting in the south.[119] Shortly before noon, E Troop, the 38th Cavalry Squadron light tank troop, began to fire on the advancing Germans in the vicinity of Hofen Hill.[120] By 4 pm, the 38th Cavalry and 47th Infantry Regiment defensive lines were on the brink of being overwhelmed. As a result, the 62nd Field Artillery Battalion received the order to fire all available guns on the advancing Germans in Hofen.[121] This artillery was successful in stopping the German penetration, and the *326th Volksgrenadier Division* then fell back to Hofen. During the night of December 18th, E

---

[118] O'Brien, "After Action Report, 38th Cavalry Reconnaissance Squadron (Mechanized), Aug 44 thru April 45," 51; Frink, Report Title Unreadable.

[119] Shehab, "Cavalry On The Shoulder," 8; Rousek, "A Short History of the 38th Cavalry Reconnaissance Squadron (Mechanized)," 14

[120] S/SGT Zudkoff, Walter, "Report of S/SGT Walter (NMI) Zudkoff 12020660, Forward Observer, Troop E, 38th CAV RCN SQ (MECZ)," in "After Action Report, 38th Cavalry Reconnaissance Squadron (Mechanized), Aug 44 thru April 45." n.d. Ike Skelton Combined Arms Research Library (CARL) Digital Library. 2011. World War II Operational Documents. May 16, 2011.

[121] Way, "Certificate," 2; O'Brien, "After Action Report, 38th Cavalry Reconnaissance Squadron (Mechanized), Aug 44 thru April 45," 55

Troop continued to fire at German vehicles near Hofen as the Germans attempted to bolster their positions.[122] The 38th Cavalry Squadron reconsolidated on Menzerath Hill as the 47th Infantry Regiment began to take control of the southern half of the Monschau sector.[123]

Throughout the entire Defense of Monschau, the 38th Cavalry Squadron miraculously only received two casualties.[124] The *326th Volksgrenadier Division* suffered substantial losses. It is difficult to determine precisely how many of the *326th Volksgrenadier Divisions* soldiers were killed or wounded at Monschau, but by December 21st they had lost 1,978 soldiers. 522 Germans had died at the hands of the 38th Cavalry between 16-17 December, and an unknown number were wounded.[125] During that

---

[122] Zudkoff, "Report of S/SGT Walter (NMI) Zudkoff 12020660, Forward Observer, Troop E, 38th CAV RCN SQ (MECZ)."

[123] Shehab, "Cavalry On The Shoulder," 8; Rousek, "A Short History of the 38th Cavalry Reconnaissance Squadron (Mechanized)," 14

[124] O'Brien, "After Action Report, 38th Cavalry Reconnaissance Squadron (Mechanized), Aug 44 thru April 45," 52

[125] SGT Messano, Martin P., "Affidavit." in "After Action Report, 38th Cavalry Reconnaissance Squadron (Mechanized), Aug 44 thru April 45." n.d. Ike Skelton Combined Arms Research Library (CARL) Digital Library. 2011. World War II Operational Documents. May 16, 2011; CPT Frink, George R., "Report of Captain George R. Frink S-2, 38th CAV. RCN. SQ (MECZ) of Dead Germans Reported by Troop C, 38th CAV. RCN. SQ. (MECZ)," in "After Action Report, 38th Cavalry Reconnaissance Squadron (Mechanized), Aug 44 thru April 45." n.d. Ike Skelton Combined Arms Research Library (CARL) Digital Library. 2011. World War II

same period, the *LXVII Corps* lost a total of 2,119 soldiers. 93% of the *LXVII Corps* casualties were from the *326ᵗʰ Volksgrenadier Division.*[126] The 38ᵗʰ Cavalry Squadron remained in the Menzerath-

---

Operational Documents. May 16, 2011; 1LT Cullinan, Robert J., "Certificate," January 18, 1945. in "After Action Report, 38th Cavalry Reconnaissance Squadron (Mechanized), Aug 44 thru April 45." n.d. Ike Skelton Combined Arms Research Library (CARL) Digital Library. 2011. World War II Operational Documents. May 16, 2011; 2LT Ketz, Howard E., "Certificate," December 17, 1944. in "After Action Report, 38th Cavalry Reconnaissance Squadron (Mechanized), Aug 44 thru April 45." n.d. Ike Skelton Combined Arms Research Library (CARL) Digital Library. 2011. World War II Operational Documents. May 16, 2011; S/SGT Bielicki, Bernard C., "Affidavit," January 18, 1945. in "After Action Report, 38th Cavalry Reconnaissance Squadron (Mechanized), Aug 44 thru April 45." n.d. Ike Skelton Combined Arms Research Library (CARL) Digital Library. 2011. World War II Operational Documents. May 16, 2011; Lindquist, "Affidavit"; SGT Okenhan, Charles E., "Affidavit," January 24, 1945. in "After Action Report, 38th Cavalry Reconnaissance Squadron (Mechanized), Aug 44 thru April 45." n.d. Ike Skelton Combined Arms Research Library (CARL) Digital Library. 2011. World War II Operational Documents. May 16, 2011; PVT Carpenter, Aaron B., "Affidavit," January 24, 1945. in "After Action Report, 38th Cavalry Reconnaissance Squadron (Mechanized), Aug 44 thru April 45." n.d. Ike Skelton Combined Arms Research Library (CARL) Digital Library. 2011. World War II Operational Documents. May 16, 2011; Tec 5 Misch, Fred T., "Affidavit," January 24, 1945. in "After Action Report, 38th Cavalry Reconnaissance Squadron (Mechanized), Aug 44 thru April 45." n.d. Ike Skelton Combined Arms Research Library (CARL) Digital Library. 2011. World War II Operational Documents. May 16, 2011; Brown, "Affidavit"; Riegel, "Affidavit."
    [126] Dupuy, *Hitler's Last Gamble: The Battle of the Bulge, December 1944-January 1945,* 476

Monschau area until January 6th, 1945.[127]

[127] Rousek, "A Short History of the 38th Cavalry Reconnaissance Squadron (Mechanized)," 14

Chapter III: Patrol Dominance

*"Give me six hours to chop down a tree and I will
spend the first four sharpening the axe."*
-President Abraham Lincoln

Upon arriving in Monschau on October 1st,
1944, COL O'Brien's priority of gaining
patrol dominance played a crucial factor in
facilitating the 38th Cavalry's success. Early patrols
allowed the 38th Cavalry to understand the terrain in
which they would fight on. Prominent terrain
features in the Monschau area are Menzerath Hill
located between Monschau and Imgenbroich, and two
east-to-west running roads. These roads connected
Monschau and Imgenbroich. The northern road had a
single distinct switchback like turn. The 38th Cavalry
named it the "hairpin turn." The southern road was
the Rohren Road. It turned back and forth, creating a
"snake" like resemblance on the map. Due to this
resemblance, the 38th Cavalry named this specific
portion of the road "Snake Road." Monschau was
surrounded by deep rocky draws running east to
northeast and getting smaller in depth to the
northeast.[128] The Monschau Forest consists of hills
and valleys with hardwood and evergreen trees. The

---

[128] O'Brien, "After Action Report, 38th Cavalry
Reconnaissance Squadron (Mechanized), Aug 44 thru April 45,"
40

dense forest limited any visibility at a distance and required that patrols be conducted on foot rather than from vehicles.[129] The useable road networks required constant maintenance from Engineers.[130] In A Troop's area, the Konzen Railroad Station had a small network of hard surface roads. The only terrain that gave the Germans a distinct advantage was in A Troop's area at Konzen. The Germans on the north end of Imgenbroich were located on a high ridge and could look down into the A Troop positions.[131] C Troop patrolling was limited due to the barren terrain between their defensive line and the German positions in Imgenbroich.[132]

Before the 38th Cavalry arrived in Monschau, the Germans roamed the entire wooded area surrounding Monschau.[133] The 38th Cavalry actively patrolled through November and December to gain patrol dominance.[134] These early patrols often resulted in small firefights or capturing prisoners of war.[135] To combat losing any soldiers, the 38th Cavalry largely patrolled at night and during hours of limited

---

[129] Leone, "In Front of the Front-Line," 38

[130] O'Brien, "After Action Report, 38th Cavalry Reconnaissance Squadron (Mechanized), Aug 44 thru April 45," 40

[131] Leone, "In Front of the Front-Line," 41

[132] O'Brien, "After Action Report, 38th Cavalry Reconnaissance Squadron (Mechanized), Aug 44 thru April 45," 41

[133] Rousek, "A Short History of the 38th Cavalry Reconnaissance Squadron (Mechanized)," 10

[134] Shehab, "Defense of Monschau by the 38th Cavalry Squadron," 1

[135] Shehab, "Cavalry On The Shoulder," 2

visibility.[136]   The patrols allowed all the battle positions along the 38th Cavalry's defensive line to see every possible German avenue of approach. During patrols, members of the 38th Cavalry identified observation posts that overlooked every potential German avenue of approach.   Another advantage of gaining patrol dominance was that the 38th Cavalry prevented the Germans from accurately knowing their positions and strength.[137] The constant patrols also allowed the 38th Cavalry to locate enemy positions and report changes in German activity.[138] In early December, A Troop conducted a series of patrols and identified German pillboxes in such great detail that they were able to know what kind of construction material of the pillboxes, the entrance, and the locations of machine-gun positions inside. A few days later, patrols confirmed and denied different suspected German pillbox locations while the 38th Cavalry attempted to gain a full understanding of the German opposition. F Company patrols discovered empty German pillboxes, leaving the 38th Cavalry to question the size of the German force in Imgenbroich. On December 10th, the *326th Volksgrenadier Division's* activity began to show signs of increased activity. While C Troop patrols were limited, the few that they were able to conduct identified the German sniper position that had been harassing them.

An A Troop patrol encountered a German patrol

---

[136] Rousek, "A Short History of the 38th Cavalry Reconnaissance Squadron (Mechanized)," 10

[137] Ross, "The Bulge: Per the 146th Engineer Combat Bn.," 1

[138] Leone, "In Front of the Front-Line," 38

west of Konzen.[139] Also, on the 10th of December, a 38th Cavalry patrol watched the *326th Volksgrenadier Division* cut down trees and lay straw on various trails. This German activity was in preparation for the Ardennes Offensive. The 38th Cavalry sent patrol reports to higher headquarters. The response the 38th Cavalry received was that the German activity was an attempt to pull US troops away from a planned Allied operation near Schmidt in the Hurtgen Forest.[140] On December 15th, every patrol across the entire 38th Cavalry defensive line reported a significant increase in German activity.[141] As night fell, the 38th Cavalry had a heightened sense of security in anticipation of a German attack.

On the morning of December 16th, the first patrol began at 6 am. As the German artillery stopped, 2nd Platoon, F Company heard a noise in front of their positions and elected to conduct a patrol. Eighteen meters into the patrol, they heard talking from German infantry.[142] C Troop also elected to conduct a patrol and identified the German movement toward their positions.[143] A 2nd Platoon, C Troop observation post, saw German movement inside the pillboxes in

---

[139] O'Brien, "After Action Report, 38th Cavalry Reconnaissance Squadron (Mechanized), Aug 44 thru April 45," 42-44

[140] Ross, "The Bulge: Per the 146th Engineer Combat Bn.," 1

[141] Shehab, "Cavalry On The Shoulder," 4

[142] Bielicki, "Report of Staff Sergeant Bernard C. Bielicki, Platoon Sergeant, 2nd Platoon, Company F, 38th CAV RCN SQ (MECZ)."

[143] O'Brien, "Report of 1st LT James J. O'Brien, Platoon Leader, 1st Platoon, Tr C," 1

Imgenbroich throughout the day.[144] The element of surprise that the Germans had hoped for, and achieved across the majority of the Allied front, was not achieved in Monschau due to the 38th Cavalry's patrol dominance. During the main attack on December 16th, German infantry was able to occupy a house, potentially using the house as an observation post for the planned main attack for the following morning. At 8:45 am, 1st Platoon, F Company sent a patrol to the house and killed the German occupiers.[145] 2nd Platoon, F Company conducted patrols throughout the morning along "Snake Road" and throughout their assigned area.[146] The afternoon of the 16th was filled with both US and German patrols, resulting in the US taking German prisoners.[147] 1st Platoon, C Troop continued to send patrols identifying other German attacks and movements in Imgenbroich.[148] As day turned into night, C Troop patrols identified new observation

---

[144] SGT West, Charles R., "Report of Sergeant Charles E. West 39127650, Platoon Sergeant, 2nd Platoon, Troop C, 38th CAV RCN SQ (MECZ)," December 16, 1944. in "After Action Report, 38th Cavalry Reconnaissance Squadron (Mechanized), Aug 44 thru April 45." n.d. Ike Skelton Combined Arms Research Library (CARL) Digital Library. 2011. World War II Operational Documents. May 16, 2011.

[145] O'Brien, "After Action Report, 38th Cavalry Reconnaissance Squadron (Mechanized), Aug 44 thru April 45," 45

[146] Messano, "Affidavit."; Bielicki, "Affidavit."

[147] O'Brien, "After Action Report, 38th Cavalry Reconnaissance Squadron (Mechanized), Aug 44 thru April 45," 46

[148] O'Brien, "Report of 1st LT James J. O'Brien, Platoon Leader, 1st Platoon, Tr C," 1

posts and night listening posts.[149] Throughout the night, C Troop listening posts continued to achieve patrol dominance by conducting smaller patrols around their immediate area. These small patrols identified German preparations, movements, and advances.[150] After the German airborne operation of dropping German paratroopers, B Troop ordered their platoons to conduct lateral patrols throughout the night.[151]

Shortly after midnight on the night of 16-17 December, 3rd Platoon C Troop conducted a patrol to establish an observation post. The observation post quickly identified 15 German infantry near F Company positions and radioed the information to F Company.[152] Starting at 4 am, early indications of the German attack were beginning to be reported by the 38th Cavalry. A C Troop observation post witnessed 65 German infantry approaching C Troop positions.[153] Understanding the importance of the communication network, C Troop sent patrols to repair communication wire, especially the damaged

---

[149] Coleman, "Report of 1st LT Raphail V. Coleman, Platoon Leader, 3rd Platoon, Troop C, 38 Cav. Rcn. Sq.," 1

[150] Tec 5 Anderson, Allen J., "Report of Tec 5 Allen J. Anderson, Troop C, 38th Cav Rcn Sq (Mecz)," in "After Action Report, 38th Cavalry Reconnaissance Squadron (Mechanized), Aug 44 thru April 45." n.d. Ike Skelton Combined Arms Research Library (CARL) Digital Library. 2011. World War II Operational Documents. May 16, 2011.

[151] Sain, "Report of Captain Joseph R. Sain 0-1030828, Troop Commander, Troop B, 38th CAV RCN SQ," 1

[152] Coleman, "Report of 1st LT Raphail V. Coleman, Platoon Leader, 3rd Platoon, Troop C, 38 Cav. Rcn. Sq.," 1

[153] Rousek, "A Short History of the 38th Cavalry Reconnaissance Squadron (Mechanized)," 12

communication wires leading to the 395[154] Infantry. By 8 am the 38th Cavalry patrols and observation posts identified the main German attack. 3rd Platoon, C Troop heard horse-drawn vehicles and movement along the hedgerows in the open fields to their east.[155] To give an early warning, 1st Platoon, C Troop, sent a patrol forward of their positions resulting in a firefight with German infantry. 1st Platoon, C Troop continued to send patrols throughout the day to identify any German movement.[156] Also, at 8 am German paratroopers began to be active behind B Troop positions. B Troop received heavy German artillery. 3rd Platoon, B Troop sent a patrol to the rear of their lines to counter the German paratrooper's attack during the artillery barrage. A 3rd Platoon patrol drove 18 German paratroopers south toward the 38th Cavalry command post.[157] A 10 am patrol by 1st Platoon, F Company near the "hairpin turn" identified and destroyed a German machine gun position approximately 275 meters in front of their

---

[154] T/4 Straigis, Anthony F., "Affidavit," January 9, 1945. in "After Action Report, 38th Cavalry Reconnaissance Squadron (Mechanized), Aug 44 thru April 45." n.d. Ike Skelton Combined Arms Research Library (CARL) Digital Library. 2011. World War II Operational Documents. May 16, 2011.

[155] Coleman, "Report of 1st LT Raphail V. Coleman, Platoon Leader, 3rd Platoon, Troop C, 38 Cav. Rcn. Sq.," 1

[156] O'Brien, "Report of 1st LT James J. O'Brien, Platoon Leader, 1st Platoon, Tr C," 1-2

[157] Sain, "Report of Captain Joseph R. Sain 0-1030828, Troop Commander, Troop B, 38th CAV RCN SQ," 1; O'Brien, "After Action Report, 38th Cavalry Reconnaissance Squadron (Mechanized), Aug 44 thru April 45," 48

defensive positions with grenades.[158]   As the main German attack began to penetrate the B Troop defensive lines, 1st Platoon B Troop protected its southern flank by utilizing continuous patrols and the use of artillery. These patrols identified two German infantry company's crossing railroad tracks moving toward other B Troop positions.[159]   As noon approached, A Company, 47th Infantry Regiment, began their patrols starting two kilometers west of B Troop to ensure that the B Troop counterattack did not have any pockets of German resistance.[160] These patrols found the German paratroopers that had been driven south by 3rd Platoon B Troop.[161]   The tank destroyers that reported to the 38th Cavalry along with A Company, 47th Infantry Regiment, began to patrol all the roads behind the main defensive line focusing on the main intersections. A Company, 47th Infantry Regiment, completed their patrolling behind B Troop at 4:45 pm.[162]   With the B Troop counterattack successful, the 38th Cavalry continued conducting

[158] Ketz, "Report of 2nd LT Ketz, Platoon Leader, 1st Platoon, Company F," 2; O'Brien, "After Action Report, 38th Cavalry Reconnaissance Squadron (Mechanized), Aug 44 thru April 45," 49

[159] Rousek, "A Short History of the 38th Cavalry Reconnaissance Squadron (Mechanized)," 13

[160] Sain, "Report of Captain Joseph R. Sain 0-1030828, Troop Commander, Troop B, 38th CAV RCN SQ," 2; O'Brien, "After Action Report, 38th Cavalry Reconnaissance Squadron (Mechanized), Aug 44 thru April 45," 50

[161] Sain, "Report of Captain Joseph R. Sain 0-1030828, Troop Commander, Troop B, 38th CAV RCN SQ," 2

[162] O'Brien, "After Action Report, 38th Cavalry Reconnaissance Squadron (Mechanized), Aug 44 thru April 45," 50-51

patrols. C Troop identified German infantry to the front of F Company and the rear of an engineer observation post and ordered a patrol to confront the enemy. These same patrols from C Troop continued, and at 5:30 pm, saw German movement toward B Troop.[163] The B Troop command post received this information, and Headquarters B Troop conducted a patrol to ambush the attacking Germans.[164] As night fell on December 17th, observation posts assisted in repelling any night attack by the Germans. At 10 pm, 2nd Platoon C Troop identified two German company's massing in anticipation of an attack. One company had managed to get 600 meters northeast of F Company, and the other German company was within 300 meters of C Troop.[165] Similarly, at 10:30 pm, B Troop observation posts heard movement in a draw resulting in 100 German infantry massing 500 meters northeast of C Troop.[166]

At 4 am on December 18th, 1st Platoon, C Troop conducted an early morning patrol around their observation posts and identified 55 German infantry.[167] As the 38th Cavalry continued to patrol

---

[163] West, "Report of Sergeant Charles E. West 39127650, Platoon Sergeant, 2nd Platoon, Troop C, 38th CAV RCN SQ (MECZ)."

[164] Sain, "Report of Captain Joseph R. Sain 0-1030828, Troop Commander, Troop B, 38th CAV RCN SQ," 2

[165] Frink, Report Title Unreadable; West, "Report of Sergeant Charles E. West 39127650, Platoon Sergeant, 2nd Platoon, Troop C, 38th CAV RCN SQ (MECZ)."

[166] Frink, Report Title Unreadable; Rousek, "A Short History of the 38th Cavalry Reconnaissance Squadron (Mechanized)," 13

[167] Anderson, "Report of Tec 5 Allen J. Anderson, Troop C, 38th Cav Rcn Sq (Mecz)."

the Monschau area, 1st Platoon, C Troop found a German observation post near their positions.[168] By 8 am a major German attack had not yet fully developed as anticipated by the 38th Cavalry. The Squadron began to focus their patrol attention on the German paratroopers. The Squadron command post continued to send patrols to secure the surrounding area from German paratroopers.[169] 3rd Platoon, F Company sent patrols to the rear of their lines looking to German paratroopers and any other Germans that had slipped through the 38th Cavalry's lines.[170] As the fight in Hofen between the 395th Infantry Regiment and the *326th Volksgrenadier Division* continued, C Troop focused their patrols to the south to ensure they maintained in contact with the 395th Infantry Regiment. C Troop patrols assisted the 395th Infantry Regiment in calling for artillery support on the attacking Germans in Hofen.[171] B Troop conducted a series of patrols throughout the day and continued into the night.[172] One of the B Troop night patrols engaged in a small-arms firefight with 14 Germans who were also conducting a patrol. B Troop was able to take one of the Germans prisoners. The German prisoner stated that the mission of the German patrol was to see if anyone occupied the

---

[168] O'Brien, "Report of 1st LT James J. O'Brien, Platoon Leader, 1st Platoon, Tr C," 2

[169] O'Brien, "After Action Report, 38th Cavalry Reconnaissance Squadron (Mechanized), Aug 44 thru April 45," 48

[170] Cullinan, "Certificate."

[171] Straigis, "Affidavit."

[172] Okenhan, "Affidavit"; Carpenter, "Affidavit,"; Misch, "Affidavit."

Konzen Railroad Station and if there were mines along the Monschau-Eupen road.[173]

---

[173] O'Brien, "After Action Report, 38th Cavalry Reconnaissance Squadron (Mechanized), Aug 44 thru April 45," 55

Chapter IV: Key Placement of Weapon Systems

"Wars may be fought with weapons, but they are won by men. It is the spirit of men who follow and of the man who leads that gains the victory."
-General George S. Patton

A s the Allies controlled the air, Hitler knew that his Ardennes Offensive would not be successful if he could not eliminate Allied air support. Because of this, Hitler chose the timing of the Ardennes Offensive to occur at a time when the weather was at its worst for flying and would render the Allied air superiority useless.[174] Due to the fog and snowstorms, Allied planes were grounded and could not support the 38th Cavalry.[175] Upon arriving in Monschau, COL O'Brien knew that the harsh winter weather was only a few weeks away, therefore making his second priority to place weapon systems in the best positions possible for his defense. The 38th Cavalry Squadron had two attachments in Monschau. A Company, 122nd Engineer Battalion, provided all the engineer support, and M10 Tank Destroyers from

---

[174] Caddick-Adams, Peter, "The Battle of the Bulge." (Power-Point presentation, Dan Hill's History from Home, March 25, 2020)
https://www.danhillmilitaryhistorian.com/archive
[175] Leone, "In Front of the Front-Line," 46

F Company, 893[176] Tank Destroyer Battalion.[176] COL O'Brien gave 3rd Platoon, A Company, 122nd Engineer the task of assisting each defensive position along the 38th Cavalry's defensive line with placing and maintaining trip flares and concertina wire.[177] The 38th Cavalry dismounted fifty .30 caliber and .50 caliber machine guns and placed them into fifty different machine gun positions.[178] Each machine gun position was dug in with overhead cover and had multiple lines of communication.[179] With the amount and variety of different tasks that the 38th Cavalry had to complete, often, each machine gun position would have a single soldier operating the machine gun, potentially for two to three hours at a time.[180] The patrols that the 38th Cavalry conducted facilitated the emplacement of observation posts, armed with small arms and multiple lines of communication throughout the entire area. These observation posts were key "weapon systems" in and of themselves as they were the forward "eyes" of the defensive line and communicated directly to the main defensive line and the supporting field artillery battalions.

By November 6th, the 38th Cavalry had focused on building and improving their battle positions, laying more concertina wire and trip flares, and ensured each

---

[176] Shehab, "Cavalry On The Shoulder," 2

[177] O'Brien, "After Action Report, 38th Cavalry Reconnaissance Squadron (Mechanized), Aug 44 thru April 45," 41

[178] Shehab, "Cavalry On The Shoulder," 3; O'Brien, "After Action Report, 38th Cavalry Reconnaissance Squadron (Mechanized), Aug 44 thru April 45," 40

[179] Shehab, "Cavalry On The Shoulder," 3

[180] Leone, "In Front of the Front-Line," 43

machine gun and tank destroyer position had clear fields of fire all along the entire defensive line.[181] The 38th Cavalry attached two F Company tank destroyers to A Troop to defend the Konzen Railroad station.[182] When the 38th Cavalry command post received word of a German armored division in Imgenbroich in early December, COL O'Brien ordered the engineers to emplace more anti-tank mines across the 38th Cavalry's sector.[183] During December, sniper fire consistently harassed C Troop positions. C Troop used its observation posts and listening post to slowly locate the German sniper position. On the morning of December 15th, C Troop placed a sharpshooter in position forward of the main defensive line and killed the German sniper as he was walking down a road to his position. Sniper fire immediately ceased in the C Troop area.[184] This German sniper could have inflicted considerable damage on C Troop during the German assault on December 16th. In the closing hours of daylight, a forward observer with B Troop saw an increase in German activity in and around Imgenbroich.[185] When

---

[181] Rousek, "A Short History of the 38th Cavalry Reconnaissance Squadron (Mechanized)," 11; O'Brien, "After Action Report, 38th Cavalry Reconnaissance Squadron (Mechanized), Aug 44 thru April 45," 41

[182] O'Brien, "After Action Report, 38th Cavalry Reconnaissance Squadron (Mechanized), Aug 44 thru April 45," 41

[183] Leone, "In Front of the Front-Line," 45

[184] O'Brien, "After Action Report, 38th Cavalry Reconnaissance Squadron (Mechanized), Aug 44 thru April 45," 43

[185] Comfort, "Certificate," 1

this report got to COL O'Brien, he ordered that an engineer platoon work throughout the night of 15-16 December and emplace more concertina wire and trip flares. The engineer platoon finished its task at 4:45 am, only 45 minutes before the start of the German Ardennes Offensive.[186]

C Troop and 2nd Platoon F Company met the brunt of the German attack on the 16th of December. At 6:00 am, *1st Battalion, 751st Regiment* attacked C Troop and 2nd Platoon F Company positions.[187] 2nd Platoon, F Company began firing machine guns and 37mm canister and high explosive rounds, from the tank destroyers main gun, after German infantry set off a single trip flare. The Germans were only 18 to 45 meters away from 2nd Platoon F Company.[188] The bulk of the German *751st Regiment* attacked down "Snake Road." Just as the German artillery and rocket barrage ceased, 1st Platoon C Troop radioed to E Troop for direct fire support at 50 advancing German infantry that was west of Menzerath.[189] At 7:30 am, a C Troop observation post identified the

---

[186] O'Brien, "After Action Report, 38th Cavalry Reconnaissance Squadron (Mechanized), Aug 44 thru April 45," 44

[187] Rousek, "A Short History of the 38th Cavalry Reconnaissance Squadron (Mechanized)," 11

[188] O'Brien, "After Action Report, 38th Cavalry Reconnaissance Squadron (Mechanized), Aug 44 thru April 45," 45; Shehab, "Cavalry On The Shoulder," 4; Bielicki, "Report of Staff Sergeant Bernard C. Bielicki, Platoon Sergeant, 2nd Platoon, Company F, 38th CAV RCN SQ (MECZ)."

[189] O'Brien, "Report of 1st LT James J. O'Brien, Platoon Leader, 1st Platoon, Tr C," 1; Zudkoff, "Report of S/SGT Walter (NMI) Zudkoff 12020660, Forward Observer, Troop E, 38th CAV RCN SQ (MECZ)."

German advance. The *751ˢᵗ Regiment* was met by a ferocious mix of small arms and machine-gun fire from 3ʳᵈ Platoon C Troop.[190] At 7:45 am, German infantry from *1ˢᵗ Battalion, 751ˢᵗ Regiment* followed a riverbed and was successful in penetrating between 2ⁿᵈ Platoon, F Company's tank sections. 2ⁿᵈ Platoon quickly identified this small penetration and moved a tank destroyer into position. The tank destroyer used its .30 caliber coaxial machine gun to stop the German penetration and kill the German infantry.[191] With the barren terrain in front of C Troop, 3ʳᵈ Platoon observed field equipped Germans moving into bunkers across from their positions in Imgenbroich and utilized a .50 caliber machine gun to fire into the German bunker causing casualties and panic among the Germans.[192] The second wave of German infantry from the *751ˢᵗ Regiment* was again sent down "Snake Road" and met by both C Troops 2ⁿᵈ and 3ʳᵈ Platoons machine guns.[193] This wave of attacking German infantry occupied a series of houses near "Snake Road." The 38ᵗʰ Cavalry slightly readjusted its tank destroyers as 2ⁿᵈ Platoon, F

---

[190] Rousek, "A Short History of the 38th Cavalry Reconnaissance Squadron (Mechanized)," 12; Coleman, "Report of 1st LT Raphail V. Coleman, Platoon Leader, 3rd Platoon, Troop C, 38 Cav. Rcn. Sq.," 1

[191] Bielicki, "Report of Staff Sergeant Bernard C. Bielicki, Platoon Sergeant, 2nd Platoon, Company F, 38th CAV RCN SQ (MECZ)."; O'Brien, "After Action Report, 38th Cavalry Reconnaissance Squadron (Mechanized), Aug 44 thru April 45," 45

[192] Coleman, "Report of 1st LT Raphail V. Coleman, Platoon Leader, 3rd Platoon, Troop C, 38 Cav. Rcn. Sq.," 1

[193] Rousek, "A Short History of the 38th Cavalry Reconnaissance Squadron (Mechanized)," 12

Company received an additional M10 tank destroyer. This newly arrived tank destroyer moved into a position to destroy the German positions along "Snake Road."[194] This repositioning of tank destroyers allowed the 38th Cavalry to destroy the buildings that the Germans were in along the road, completely denying any chance the *751st Regiment* had of obtaining forward positions.[195] At 10 am, E Troop was again radioed by C Troop to fire at 20 German infantry directly in front of C Troop positions.[196] An engineer platoon arrived at a 2nd Platoon, F Company tank destroyer positions around 2 pm, and placed boobytraps along different avenues of approach from Menzerath Hill.[197] In an attempt to assist in the defensive line, six additional machine gun crews from the 186th Field Artillery Battalion and another M10 tank destroyer were sent to 2nd Platoon F Company. E Troop fired 760 rounds throughout the day, mostly in the area in front of C Troop.[198]

---

[194] Bielicki, "Report of Staff Sergeant Bernard C. Bielicki, Platoon Sergeant, 2nd Platoon, Company F, 38th CAV RCN SQ (MECZ)."

[195] O'Brien, "After Action Report, 38th Cavalry Reconnaissance Squadron (Mechanized), Aug 44 thru April 45," 45

[196] Zudkoff, "Report of S/SGT Walter (NMI) Zudkoff 12020660, Forward Observer, Troop E, 38th CAV RCN SQ (MECZ)."

[197] Bielicki, "Report of Staff Sergeant Bernard C. Bielicki, Platoon Sergeant, 2nd Platoon, Company F, 38th CAV RCN SQ (MECZ)."

[198] Bielicki, "Report of Staff Sergeant Bernard C. Bielicki, Platoon Sergeant, 2nd Platoon, Company F, 38th CAV RCN SQ (MECZ)."; Rousek, "A Short History of the 38th Cavalry Reconnaissance Squadron (Mechanized)," 12; 1LT

On December 17th at 4 am, a C Troop observation post identified 65 Germans approaching and received supporting fire from E Troop's light tanks.[199] As the German morning attack began on the 38th Cavalry's defensive positions, 2nd Platoon B Troop, emplaced two .30 caliber machine guns, one .50 caliber machine gun, and two tank destroyers overlooking an anticipated German avenue of approach.[200] By 7:15 am 3rd Platoon, F Company employed all its tanks to repel advancing German infantry.[201] The amount of fire that 3rd Platoon F Company placed on the Germans turned them north into B Troop. At 7:45 am, 3rd Platoon observed and placed accurate .30 caliber machine gun and 37mm canister fire into the flank of German infantry advancing on B Troop positions.[202] 3rd Platoon was also able to observe German infantry along the railroad tracks but was out

Allen, Albert C., "Missions fired by Troop E, 38th Cav Rcn Sq (Mecz) from 160600A December 1944 to 170600A December 1944," in "After Action Report, 38th Cavalry Reconnaissance Squadron (Mechanized), Aug 44 thru April 45." n.d. Ike Skelton Combined Arms Research Library (CARL) Digital Library. 2011. World War II Operational Documents. May 16, 2011, 1

[199] O'Brien, "After Action Report, 38th Cavalry Reconnaissance Squadron (Mechanized), Aug 44 thru April 45," 47; Rousek, "A Short History of the 38th Cavalry Reconnaissance Squadron (Mechanized)," 12

[200] Yontz, "Report of 1st LT. W. J. Yontz, Platoon Leader, 2nd Platoon, Troop B, Action of 17 December 1944," 1

[201] O'Brien, "After Action Report, 38th Cavalry Reconnaissance Squadron (Mechanized), Aug 44 thru April 45," 47

[202] Cullinan, "Report of 1st LT. Robert J. Cullinan 1032424 Platoon Leader, 3rd Platoon, Company F, 38th CAV RCN SQ," 1

of range to engage them. 3rd Platoon informed 1st Platoon F Company, located with A Troop, to use small arms fire and kill the German infantry along the railroad tracks.[203] Again, the *326th Volksgrenadier Division* sent a regiment down "Snake Road" and into C Troop. The German advance was quickly executed and large enough that 3rd Platoon C Troop was unable to stop the advance alone. Both 1st Platoon and 3rd Platoon C Troop engaged the Germans with both .30 and .50 caliber machine guns. 3rd Platoon F Company joined the firefight and added the necessary firepower and weapon systems needed to stop the German advance.[204] At 8:30 am, 2nd Platoon F Company fired at German Infantry advancing from Menzerath Hill.[205] With the German attack mounting against B Troop, 3rd Platoon F Company began to fire 37mm main gun rounds, and both .30 caliber coaxial and .50 caliber machine guns at the flank of the German infantry attacking B Troop.[206] By 8:45 am a platoon of German infantry were in the woods across from B Troop and at a range to close for artillery support, signaling the beginning of the German

---

[203] Ketz, "Report of 2nd LT Ketz, Platoon Leader, 1st Platoon, Company F," 1

[204] Rousek, "A Short History of the 38th Cavalry Reconnaissance Squadron (Mechanized)," 12; O'Brien, "Report of 1st LT James J. O'Brien, Platoon Leader, 1st Platoon, Tr C," 1; Coleman, "Report of 1st LT Raphail V. Coleman, Platoon Leader, 3rd Platoon, Troop C, 38 Cav. Rcn. Sq.," 1

[205] O'Brien, "After Action Report, 38th Cavalry Reconnaissance Squadron (Mechanized), Aug 44 thru April 45," 48

[206] Cullinan, "Report of 1st LT. Robert J. Cullinan 1032424 Platoon Leader, 3rd Platoon, Company F, 38th CAV RCN SQ," 1

penetration of B Troop positions.[207]

2nd Platoon B Troop began to receive small arms fire from the north end of their defensive positions and placed a personnel carrier with machine guns in position to fire on a small group of Germans, forcing them to flee north.[208] Simultaneously, 2nd Platoon F Company fired 37mm main gun at German mortar positions firing on B Troop at a range of 820 meters.[209] The *326th Volksgrenadier Division* continued to fire rockets and artillery in support of their advance on B Troop. As German artillery and rockets burst around B Troop positions, 3rd Platoon F Company, in armored tank destroyers, continued to fire along the railroad tracks in an attempt to limit the advance of the German infantry.[210] By 9 am, C Troop began to observe German infantry in Imgenbroich beginning to move into positions to reinforce the German penetration. All C Troop machine guns and F Company tank destroyers near the C Troop lines fired at the advancing German infantry and houses they occupied along the way. The 38th Cavalry's anti-aircraft batteries fired over C Troop positions directly at massing German infantry. E Troop's light

[207] Ketz, "Report of 2nd LT Ketz, Platoon Leader, 1st Platoon, Company F," 1

[208] Yontz, "Report of 1st LT. W. J. Yontz, Platoon Leader, 2nd Platoon, Troop B, Action of 17 December 1944," 1

[209] O'Brien, "After Action Report, 38th Cavalry Reconnaissance Squadron (Mechanized), Aug 44 thru April 45," 48

[210] Cullinan, "Report of 1st LT. Robert J. Cullinan 1032424 Platoon Leader, 3rd Platoon, Company F, 38th CAV RCN SQ," 1; Gier, "Report of Joseph C. Gier 32583371, 3rd Platoon, Company F, 38th CAV RCN SQ (MECZ)."

tanks attempted to slow the German march by firing at Germans east of 1st Platoon F Company and along "Snake Road."[211] The F Company tanks fired 37mm high explosive rounds at German positions until they were almost out of high explosive ammunition. The Germans returned fire with mortars and heavy machine guns from pillboxes at ranges less than 550 meters. The exchange between the Germans, C Troop, and F Company lasted for more than an hour. 3rd Platoon, F Company focused on destroying the German mortar positions, and by 11 am, 1st Platoon F Company fired 37mm high explosive rounds at German pillboxes and machine-gun positions and continued until the German guns became silent.[212] Near the end of this firefight, the situation along the B Troop defensive line became dire, and F Company

---

[211] Zudkoff, "Report of S/SGT Walter (NMI) Zudkoff 12020660, Forward Observer, Troop E, 38th CAV RCN SQ (MECZ).")"; MAJ Rousek, Charles E., "Defense of Monschau." June 23, 2012. http://battleofthebulgememories.be/stories26/us-army25/648-defense-of-monschau.html, 5

[212] Coleman, "Report of 1st LT Raphail V. Coleman, Platoon Leader, 3rd Platoon, Troop C, 38 Cav. Rcn. Sq.," 1; O'Brien, "After Action Report, 38th Cavalry Reconnaissance Squadron (Mechanized), Aug 44 thru April 45," 48, 50; Ketz, "Report of 2nd LT Ketz, Platoon Leader, 1st Platoon, Company F," 1; Cullinan, "Report of 1st LT. Robert J. Cullinan 1032424 Platoon Leader, 3rd Platoon, Company F, 38th CAV RCN SQ," 1; S/SGT Lindquist, Kenneth C., "Report of Staff Sergeant Kenneth C. Lindquist, Platoon Sergeant, 3rd Platoon, Company F, 38th CAV RCN SQ (MECZ)" December 17, 1944. in "After Action Report, 38th Cavalry Reconnaissance Squadron (Mechanized), Aug 44 thru April 45." n.d. Ike Skelton Combined Arms Research Library (CARL) Digital Library. 2011. World War II Operational Documents. May 16, 2011.

dispatched two tanks to support B Troop.[213]

As the German penetration mounted and began to overrun positions, B Troop withdrew their attached tank destroyers beginning at 9:45 am.[214] The tank destroyers fell back to secondary battle positions and covered the retreat of any remaining B Troop soldiers. By mid-morning, the Germans added another element to the German penetration that the Allies could not answer. 20 Me-109 German fighters appeared from the east and attacked 38th Cavalry positions. The Me-109 fighters focused strafing on B Troop positions until a B Troop armored personnel carrier at the B Troop command post used a .50 caliber machine gun to set a German fighter on fire, that crashed east of Imgenbroich.[215] At 11 am, the last B Troop tank destroyer and machine-gun positions were pulled back from the main defensive line.[216] Just as the last B Troop soldiers and weapons were falling back into alternate defensive positions, A Company, 47th Infantry Regiment, reported to the Squadron command post. The tank destroyers attached to A Company, 47th Infantry Regiment, began to control the road intersections throughout the 38th Cavalry area, and by 11:30 am had secured the main routes ensuring that supplies remained

---

[213] Ketz, "Report of 2nd LT Ketz, Platoon Leader, 1st Platoon, Company F," 2

[214] Comfort, "Certificate," 1

[215] Sain, "Report of Captain Joseph R. Sain 0-1030828, Troop Commander, Troop B, 38th CAV RCN SQ," 2; Rousek, "A Short History of the 38th Cavalry Reconnaissance Squadron (Mechanized)," 13

[216] Yontz, "Report of 1st LT. W. J. Yontz, Platoon Leader, 2nd Platoon, Troop B, Action of 17 December 1944," 1

continuous from Eupen.[217]

As B Troop and the 38th Cavalry conducted the counterattack, F Company remained in contact with the Germans attempting to exploit the German penetration, and E Troop fired heavy defensive fires in the area of German penetration.[218] 3rd Platoon, F Company spotted German machine gun crews and infantry and fired 37mm high explosive rounds at ranges as close as 100 meters. B Troop observation posts utilized E Troop to destroy German machine gun positions, assisting in the counterattack.[219] At noon, four German Mark IV tanks, with infantry support, were identified by 38th Cavalry observation posts. E Troop and the 186th Field Artillery Battalion destroyed the tanks.[220] By 2:45 pm, the B Troop counterattack was successful and identified any remaining pockets of German resistance. B Troop

---

[217] O'Brien, "After Action Report, 38th Cavalry Reconnaissance Squadron (Mechanized), Aug 44 thru April 45," 50

[218] O'Brien, "After Action Report, 38th Cavalry Reconnaissance Squadron (Mechanized), Aug 44 thru April 45," 51

[219] S/SGT Fisher, William F., "Report of S/SGT William F. Fisher, 35438173, Forward Observer, Troop B, 38th Cav Rcn Sq," in "After Action Report, 38th Cavalry Reconnaissance Squadron (Mechanized), Aug 44 thru April 45." n.d. Ike Skelton Combined Arms Research Library (CARL) Digital Library. 2011. World War II Operational Documents. May 16, 2011.

[220] Shehab, "Cavalry On The Shoulder," 8; Rousek, "A Short History of the 38th Cavalry Reconnaissance Squadron (Mechanized)," 12-13; Zudkoff, "Report of S/SGT Walter (NMI) Zudkoff 12020660, Forward Observer, Troop E, 38th CAV RCN SQ (MECZ)."

forward observers continued to observe German infantry along roads and received support from E Troop.[221] Once again, 3rd Platoon, F Company used 37mm high explosive rounds and .30 caliber machine gun fire to thwart any remaining advancing Germans on B Troop.[222] Once B Troop solidified their positions after the counterattack, they received a company of M4 Sherman tanks in support of their defensive line.[223] During the lull in the days battle, the 38th Cavalry distributed much-needed ammunition.[224] Between 3-5 pm, German infantry attempted to withdraw back to Imgenbroich and were seen by B Troop and 3rd Platoon F Company who fired their machine guns at the withdrawing German infantry. Many of the withdrawing Germans were pinned down by the machine-gun fire and killed by artillery fire.[225] At 5 pm, a forward observer with the 186th Field Artillery Battalion, near C Troop positions, identified a German Battalion moving west

---

[221] Fisher, "Report of S/SGT William F. Fisher, 35438173, Forward Observer, Troop B, 38th Cav Rcn Sq."

[222] Cullinan, "Report of 1st LT. Robert J. Cullinan 1032424 Platoon Leader, 3rd Platoon, Company F, 38th CAV RCN SQ," 1; Lindquist, "Report of Staff Sergeant Kenneth C. Lindquist, Platoon Sergeant, 3rd Platoon, Company F, 38th CAV RCN SQ (MECZ)."

[223] Sain, "Report of Captain Joseph R. Sain 0-1030828, Troop Commander, Troop B, 38th CAV RCN SQ," 2

[224] Ketz, "Report of 2nd LT Ketz, Platoon Leader, 1st Platoon, Company F," 2

[225] Cullinan, "Report of 1st LT. Robert J. Cullinan 1032424 Platoon Leader, 3rd Platoon, Company F, 38th CAV RCN SQ," 2; O'Brien, "After Action Report, 38th Cavalry Reconnaissance Squadron (Mechanized), Aug 44 thru April 45," 51

from Imgenbroich along the hedgerows in front of C Troop. The German battalion was deliberate in their movement and was slow in their advance. At 8 pm, the Germans were within range, and 2nd Platoon, C Troop engaged the German Battalion with machine guns and light tank fire from E Troop[226]. Two 57mm guns from the 47th Infantry Regiment, who arrived in Monschau around 5 pm, were put into positions near C Troop. The two 57mm guns were ordered to stay in place and assist C Troop in defeating any German advance out of Imgenbroich.[227] During the night, both B and C Troops identified advancing German infantry and used E Troop's light tanks to defeat the attacks. A C Troop observation post identified 200 German infantry, and E Troop immediately fired, killing most of the Germans and began walking their rounds up "Snake Road" in 45-meter intervals. A short time later, a B Troop observation post similarly heard German movement, and the resulting illumination rounds revealed 100 Germans. E Troop fired over 150 rounds to stop this German advance.[228]

---

[226] West, "Report of Sergeant Charles E. West 39127650, Platoon Sergeant, 2nd Platoon, Troop C, 38th CAV RCN SQ (MECZ)."

[227] Rousek, "A Short History of the 38th Cavalry Reconnaissance Squadron (Mechanized)," 13; Rogers, "Report of Capitan Elmer L. Rogers, Commanding Officer, Troop C, 38th CAV RCN SQ (MECZ)."; West, "Report of Sergeant Charles E. West 39127650, Platoon Sergeant, 2nd Platoon, Troop C, 38th CAV RCN SQ (MECZ)."; O'Brien, "After Action Report, 38th Cavalry Reconnaissance Squadron (Mechanized), Aug 44 thru April 45," 51

[228] Rousek, "A Short History of the 38th Cavalry Reconnaissance Squadron (Mechanized)," 13; O'Brien, "After Action Report, 38th Cavalry Reconnaissance Squadron

In the early hours of 18 December, an engineer platoon completed emplacing a minefield in front of the B Troop defensive line in anticipation of another German attack.[229] The 47th Infantry Regiment started taking control of the southern half of the 38th Cavalry's defensive line. They start by relieving C Troop and elements of F Company. E Troop fired over 900 rounds at German infantry during the transition.[230]

The placement of the machine gun positions, observation posts, and tank destroyers proved pivotal in the 38th Cavalry's successful defense of Monschau. The number of weapons and firepower that C Troop and F Company were able to bear down upon the Germans attempting to reinforce elements already attacking B Troop, deterred the *326th Volksgrenadier Division* from exploiting the penetration. Furthermore, it gave the B Troop counterattack the time necessary to occupy and call for artillery on any remaining German reinforcements. The .50 caliber machine gun was the only weapon system that the 38th Cavalry had in the vicinity of B Troop that could inflict damage on a German Me-109 fighter. Had B Troop not been able to have a .50 caliber to fire at the

---

(Mechanized), Aug 44 thru April 45," 52; Zudkoff, "Report of S/SGT Walter (NMI) Zudkoff 12020660, Forward Observer, Troop E, 38th CAV RCN SQ (MECZ)."; Rousek, "Defense of Monschau," 5

[229] O'Brien, "After Action Report, 38th Cavalry Reconnaissance Squadron (Mechanized), Aug 44 thru April 45," 52

[230] Allen, "Missions fired by Troop E, 38th Cav Rcn Sq (Mecz) from 160600A December 1944 to 170600A December 1944," 2

German fighter planes, the Me-109s would have likely continued to wreak havoc on B Troop, ensuring the German penetration held, thus cutting A Troop off from the 38th Cavalry Squadron. The arrival of the tank destroyer platoon with the 47th Infantry Regiment allowed the 38th Cavalry to secure the rear area and focus on the German penetration. The 38th Cavalry Squadron's Executive Officer believed that the success of the entire defense depended on grazing machine-gun fire and artillery support.[231]

---

[231] Rousek, "A Short History of the 38th Cavalry Reconnaissance Squadron (Mechanized)," 10

Chapter V: Artillery Support

"If you don't have enough artillery, quit."
-General Richards Cavasos

In direct support of the 38th Cavalry Squadron was their organic 60mm and 81mm mortars, and the 62nd Field Artillery Battalion. The 186th and 955th Field Artillery Battalions were also in supporting range of the 38th Cavalry.[232] The 62nd and 186th Field Artillery Battalions were in the Monschau area, but the 186th Field Artillery Battalion was for deep artillery support of the 38th Cavalry. The 186th Field Artillery Battalion only fired two artillery missions within one kilometer of the 38th Cavalry.[233] The majority of the field artillery battalions had moved into positions around Monschau on December 12th and 13th, to include the 496th Field Artillery Group, in anticipation of the US V Corps offensive operation to seize the Roer River dams.[234] A 155mm artillery

---

[232] Shehab, "Cavalry On The Shoulder," 4

[233] MAJ Fingerhut, R. V., "Fires: Extract," in "After Action Report, 38th Cavalry Reconnaissance Squadron (Mechanized), Aug 44 thru April 45." n.d. Ike Skelton Combined Arms Research Library (CARL) Digital Library. 2011. World War II Operational Documents. May 16, 2011.

[234] Rousek, "A Short History of the 38th Cavalry Reconnaissance Squadron (Mechanized)," 11; O'Brien, "After Action Report, 38th Cavalry Reconnaissance Squadron (Mechanized), Aug 44 thru April 45," 43

battalion was placed less than a kilometer behind C Troop and in front of the C Troop's mortar position. Having the proximity of the artillery battalions facilitated Allied unobserved harassing fires nightly on German positions.[235] German personnel targets were limited in the days leading up to the Ardennes Offensive due to the German concrete fortifications.[236] The 38th Cavalry anticipated the importance of artillery support in the weeks leading up to the Ardennes Offensive, resulting in the 38th Cavalry ensuring that every soldier trained on the employment and use of 81mm mortars.[237]

On December 16th, supporting field artillery units fired a total of 1,478 rounds in support of the 38th Cavalry.[238] Just as the German artillery and rocket barrage ceased, 2nd Platoon F Company utilized C Troop mortars to disrupt the German advance. C Troop fired 60mm illumination rounds that help 2nd Platoon observe 70 Germans advancing on their positions.[239] The main German assault began to materialize as they advanced down "Snake Road" and at 8:30 am, C Troop called the 62nd Field Artillery

---

[235] O'Brien, "After Action Report, 38th Cavalry Reconnaissance Squadron (Mechanized), Aug 44 thru April 45," 43

[236] Way, "Certificate," 1

[237] O'Brien, "After Action Report, 38th Cavalry Reconnaissance Squadron (Mechanized), Aug 44 thru April 45," 42

[238] Way, "Certificate," 1; Fingerhut, "Fires: Extract."

[239] O'Brien, "After Action Report, 38th Cavalry Reconnaissance Squadron (Mechanized), Aug 44 thru April 45," 45; Bielicki, "Report of Staff Sergeant Bernard C. Bielicki, Platoon Sergeant, 2nd Platoon, Company F, 38th CAV RCN SQ (MECZ)."

Battalion for artillery fire.[240] The height of the artillery support of December 16th manifested itself around noon when 2nd Platoon F Company identified 70 German infantry. The resulting artillery support pinned down the German infantry allowing both C Troop and F Company positions to repel the German attack.[241] 1st Platoon, C Troop requested artillery harassing fire throughout the day on German positions to deter the Germans from attacking Monschau.[242] Throughout the day, German personnel targets began to appear more frequently in the vicinity of Imgenbroich and Konzen, resulting in accurate artillery fire. As December 16th came to an end, the supporting artillery battalions fired 718 artillery rounds in support of the 38th Cavalry, mostly coming from the 62nd Field Artillery Battalion.[243]

Just after midnight on the night of December 16th and 17th, F Company radioed for artillery support on German infantry.[244] As daylight appeared, the B Troop Fire Support Officer identified German machine gun positions and used artillery fire to destroy them.[245] By 8 am, the 62nd Field Artillery

---

[240] Rousek, "A Short History of the 38th Cavalry Reconnaissance Squadron (Mechanized)," 12

[241] Bielicki, "Report of Staff Sergeant Bernard C. Bielicki, Platoon Sergeant, 2nd Platoon, Company F, 38th CAV RCN SQ (MECZ)."; O'Brien, "After Action Report, 38th Cavalry Reconnaissance Squadron (Mechanized), Aug 44 thru April 45," 46

[242] O'Brien, "Report of 1st LT James J. O'Brien, Platoon Leader, 1st Platoon, Tr C," 1

[243] Way, "Certificate," 1

[244] Coleman, "Report of 1st LT Raphail V. Coleman, Platoon Leader, 3rd Platoon, Troop C, 38 Cav. Rcn. Sq.," 1

[245] Comfort, "Certificate," 1

Battalion fired on German positions near C Troop. 1st Platoon, C Troop identified 50 attacking German infantry and 3rd Platoon, C Troop heard horse-drawn equipment with both C Troop Platoons received artillery fire.[246] At 9 am, 3rd Platoon, C Troop continued to receive artillery support as 50 Germans attacked their positions.[247] The German penetration of the B Troop lines began to take most of the field artillery battalions focus. The B Troop Fire Support Officer called for artillery on advancing German infantry only 450 meters from his position and continued to do so throughout the battle.[248] 2nd Platoon, B Troop also observed German infantry moving west, but with German artillery directly firing at the 38th Cavalry in support of the German advance from Imgenbroich.[249] From 10:00-10:30 am the 62nd Field Artillery Battalion fired in an attempt to break up the German attack on C Troop.[250]

With the Germans penetrating the B Troop lines, the B Troop Fire Support Officer reported that Germans were nearing his observation post to the 62nd Field Artillery Battalion. The 62nd Field Artillery Battalion dispatched two air observation posts to

---

[246] O'Brien, "Report of 1st LT James J. O'Brien, Platoon Leader, 1st Platoon, Tr C," 1

[247] Coleman, "Report of 1st LT Raphail V. Coleman, Platoon Leader, 3rd Platoon, Troop C, 38 Cav. Rcn. Sq.," 1

[248] Comfort, "Certificate," 1; Way, "Certificate," 1

[249] Fisher, "Report of S/SGT William F. Fisher, 35438173, Forward Observer, Troop B, 38th Cav Rcn Sq."

[250] O'Brien, "After Action Report, 38th Cavalry Reconnaissance Squadron (Mechanized), Aug 44 thru April 45," 49

assist in calling and adjusting artillery fire.[251] 3rd Platoon, B Troop reported that German infantry was between their positions and 1st Platoon B Troop and requested artillery support. Within 11 minutes, the 62nd Field Artillery Battalion could move the 155mm guns into position to fire on the two German company's attacking the gap between the B Troop platoons.[252] As the 38th Cavalry Squadron gathered elements to assist with the B Troop counterattack, the 62nd Field Artillery Battalion fired a smokescreen to hide the movement of the 38th Cavalry's reinforcements.[253] 1st Platoon, B Troop protected its southern flank during the German penetration with constant artillery fire.[254] During the 38th Cavalry's counterattack, the 62nd Field Artillery Battalion fired heavy defensive fires in the area of German penetration.[255] At noon, 38th Cavalry observation posts identified four German Mark IV tanks with infantry support. The 62nd Field Artillery Battalion then marked the tank targets with artillery for Allied fighter bombers.[256] The 186th Field Artillery Battalion fired artillery and destroyed three of the

---

[251] Way, "Certificate," 2

[252] O'Brien, "After Action Report, 38th Cavalry Reconnaissance Squadron (Mechanized), Aug 44 thru April 45," 50

[253] Way, "Certificate," 2

[254] Rousek, "A Short History of the 38th Cavalry Reconnaissance Squadron (Mechanized)," 13

[255] O'Brien, "After Action Report, 38th Cavalry Reconnaissance Squadron (Mechanized), Aug 44 thru April 45," 51

[256] Way, "Certificate," 2

tanks.[257]   As B Troop regained their original defensive positions, they identified approximately 75 German reinforcements, and the ensuing artillery prevented the reinforcements from reaching the German penetration.[258]

With the original 38th Cavalry defensive line re-established, B Troop forward observers continued to identify German infantry along roads and received artillery support. At 4:00 pm 3rd Platoon, F Company had pinned down German infantry but was unable to kill the Germans due to terrain. 3rd Platoon received artillery fire on the pinned German positions.[259] Artillery fire from the 186th Field Artillery Battalion stopped the last major German advance on December 17th. At 5 pm, several German company's attacked west, but the 38th Cavalry anticipated all of the routes. The 186th Field Artillery Battalion fired all 18 guns to stop the German advance.[260] A total of 2,145 rounds were fired in support of action seen on December

[257] Shehab, "Cavalry On The Shoulder," 8; Rousek, "A Short History of the 38th Cavalry Reconnaissance Squadron (Mechanized)," 12-13; Zudkoff, "Report of S/SGT Walter (NMI) Zudkoff 12020660, Forward Observer, Troop E, 38th CAV RCN SQ (MECZ)."

[258] O'Brien, "After Action Report, 38th Cavalry Reconnaissance Squadron (Mechanized), Aug 44 thru April 45," 49; Sain, "Report of Captain Joseph R. Sain 0-1030828, Troop Commander, Troop B, 38th CAV RCN SQ," 2

[259] Cullinan, "Report of 1st LT. Robert J. Cullinan 1032424 Platoon Leader, 3rd Platoon, Company F, 38th CAV RCN SQ," 2

[260] Yontz, "Report of 1st LT. W. J. Yontz, Platoon Leader, 2nd Platoon, Troop B, Action of 17 December 1944," 1; Shehab, "Cavalry On The Shoulder," 8; Frink, Report Title Unreadable.

17th. The 62nd Field Artillery Battalion fired over 1,900 rounds of 155mm in support of the 38th Cavalry.[261]

Even though the 38th Cavalry Squadron's defensive line was relatively quiet compared to the two previous days, the Field Artillery units fired in support of the 395th Infantry Regiment's defense in Hofen, Germany. At 5:10 am, C Troop identified 55 German infantry advancing on F Company and radioed for artillery fire.[262] C Troop again placed artillery fire on advancing Germans to the front of their positions at 8:14 am. As the *326th Volksgrenadier Division* began their assault on Hofen, field artillery units in support of the 38th Cavalry, fired to the south of the 38th Cavalry's defensive line to stop the German penetration in Hofen. At 4:15 pm, the field artillery units in Monschau fired all available artillery on the German penetration near Hofen.[263] The 38th Cavalry Squadron had Germans to their east and now the south as they maintained vigilant. During the night, 2nd Platoon F Company radioed for artillery on 100 German infantry approaching their positions. With the 47th Infantry Regiment relieving the 38th Cavalry along the southern end of the 38th Cavalry's defensive line, the 62nd Field Artillery Battalion continued to provide the main 155mm artillery support for the 38th Cavalry and fired over 1,800 rounds on December

---

[261] Way, "Certificate," 2; Fingerhut, "Fires: Extract."

[262] Anderson, "Report of Tec 5 Allen J. Anderson, Troop C, 38th Cav Rcn Sq (Mecz)."

[263] O'Brien, "After Action Report, 38th Cavalry Reconnaissance Squadron (Mechanized), Aug 44 thru April 45," 55

18th.[264]

---

[264] Way, "Certificate," 2

Chapter VI: Victory Lies in Communication

"If you're going through hell, keep going."
-Winston Churchill

In conjunction with establishing patrol dominance, another priority for COL O'Brien upon arriving in Monschau was establishing a robust communication network.[265] In the weeks before the Ardennes Offensive that the 38th Cavalry occupied Monschau, they built a communication network consisting of 60 radios with 16 different nets. The 38th Cavalry Squadron also employed 65 field telephones and over 50 miles of telephone wire tied to six switchboards.[266] The 38th Cavalry doubled the number of telephones and radios to all platoons, command posts, observation posts, and machine-gun positions.[267] COL O'Brien described the communication network as an elaborate wire communication network, supported by radios that linked to all units and outposts, the US V Corps and 102nd Cavalry Group headquarters, every supporting

---

[265] O'Brien, "After Action Report, 38th Cavalry Reconnaissance Squadron (Mechanized), Aug 44 thru April 45," 40

[266] Shehab, "Cavalry On The Shoulder," 3

[267] Rousek, "A Short History of the 38th Cavalry Reconnaissance Squadron (Mechanized)," 11

artillery unit, and all adjacent units.[268] Wire communication became the preferred choice of communication, but the night observation posts and patrols carried radios when going forward of the 38th Cavalry's main defensive line.[269]

Maintenance of the telephone wire required constant repair throughout the Defense of Monschau. The 38th Cavalry knew how important and vital the communication network was to the overall defensive plan. The early German artillery and rocket barrage on December 16th severely damaged the telephone wire used for wire communication. 2nd Platoon, F Company immediately lost wire communication at 5:30 am but was able to maintain radio communication and had the telephone wire repaired by 6 am.[270] While German artillery and rockets fell across the 38th Cavalry front, soldiers were out repairing the communication wire. German artillery significantly added to the complexity and difficulty of the battle for the 38th Cavalry. German artillery cut both A and B Troop wire communication lines. The German artillery on the morning of December 16th left A Troop having one operational radio that could

---

[268] O'Brien, "After Action Report, 38th Cavalry Reconnaissance Squadron (Mechanized), Aug 44 thru April 45," 40

[269] Anderson, "Report of Tec 5 Allen J. Anderson, Troop C, 38th Cav Rcn Sq (Mecz)."

[270] Bielicki, "Report of Staff Sergeant Bernard C. Bielicki, Platoon Sergeant, 2nd Platoon, Company F, 38th CAV RCN SQ (MECZ)."

communicate with one B Troop radio.[271]   B Troop
had to relay all of A Troop transmissions to the
Squadron headquarters.[272]   A Troop was nearly "cut
off" in terms of communication from the 38th
Cavalry. The only form of communication B Troop
had with the Squadron command post was by the B
Troop Fire Support Officer, who was in radio contact
with the Squadron Fire Support Officer.[273] Even as B
Troop was relaying A Troop transmissions, B Troop
gave a personnel carrier to E Troop, who had lost all
forms of communication in the early morning artillery
attack.[274]   E Troop utilized the vehicle to maintain
communication with their higher headquarters as E
Troop relayed artillery fire missions through the C
Troop command post.[275] The German artillery attack
on the morning of December 16th nearly crippled the
38th Cavalry's communication network. The
maintenance of the communication network was
constant. On the morning of December 17th, the B
Troop Fire Support Officer could hear telephone
reports from different observation posts and radioed
for artillery on German machine gun positions.[276]

---

[271] O'Brien, "After Action Report, 38th Cavalry
Reconnaissance Squadron (Mechanized), Aug 44 thru April 45,"
44

[272] Sain, "Report of Captain Joseph R. Sain 0-1030828,
Troop Commander, Troop B, 38th CAV RCN SQ," 1

[273] Comfort, "Certificate," 1

[274] Sain, "Report of Captain Joseph R. Sain 0-1030828,
Troop Commander, Troop B, 38th CAV RCN SQ," 1

[275] Zudkoff, "Report of S/SGT Walter (NMI) Zudkoff
12020660, Forward Observer, Troop E, 38th CAV RCN SQ
(MECZ)."

[276] Comfort, "Certificate," 1

The German artillery not only effected communication within the 38th Cavalry but also with the 395th Infantry Regiment. At 3 am on December 18th, all communications with the 395th Infantry Regiment was severed due to the German artillery attack on Hofen in anticipation of their assault later that morning.[277] Having seen German movement toward the south of the 38th Cavalry defensive line, C Troop dispatched patrols to repair and ensure wire communication with the 395th Infantry Regiment was working. Members of the C Troop patrol then reported the situation in Hofen and called for artillery support utilizing the wire communication network built by the 38th Cavalry.[278]

The soldiers of the 38th Cavalry's constant repairs to telephone wire, and the redundant network facilitated the flow of information during German attacks. As a communication "node" became unable to talk to higher headquarters, soldiers at the position could still reach someone else along the 38th Cavalry's defensive line. This spiderweb-like network facilitated each position in having multiple different communication options. The sheer number of accurate artillery fire displays the importance and success the communication network had on the Defense of Monschau.

---

[277] O'Brien, "After Action Report, 38th Cavalry Reconnaissance Squadron (Mechanized), Aug 44 thru April 45," 53

[278] Straigis, "Affidavit."

Chapter VII: Final Words

"I do not pilfer victory."
-Alexander the Great

The Allies were able to hold along the northern shoulder due to the success of the 38th Cavalry Squadron at Monschau. Veterans of the Defense of Monschau believe that had the 38th Cavalry fallen to the Germans along the northern shoulder, the German *6th Panzer Army* would have been able to secure vital fuel supply depots and achieve Hitler's operational objective of reaching Antwerp.[279] The lack of Allied combat units capable of stopping the German *LXVII Corps* behind the 38th Cavalry Squadron highlights how differently the Ardennes Offensive could have been. The entire Allied logistical infrastructure would have been at risk. Even if the German *6th Panzer Army* not been able to reach Antwerp, or even Eupen, the control of the Konzen Railroad station would have provided the German military a significant logistical point to store and quickly move supplies throughout the Ardennes Region. After the Ardennes Offensive, during his interrogation, a German major who was a prisoner of

---

[279] Rousek, "A Short History of the 38th Cavalry Reconnaissance Squadron (Mechanized)," 11; Leone, "In Front of the Front-Line," 47; Shehab, "Cavalry On The Shoulder," 4; Ross, "The Bulge: Per the 146th Engineer Combat Bn.," 3

war was asked why he believed the Ardennes Offensive failed. He answered, "we failed because our right flank near Monschau ran its head against a wall."[280] COL O'Brien's forethought and priorities directly attributed to the 38th Cavalry Squadrons' ability to come out victorious against the *326th Volksgrenadier Division* and the *LXVII Corps*. He did not always follow US Army doctrine but made the best of his situation and circumstances. He gained the respect of his subordinates. Many times, during the Defense of Monschau, the 38th Cavalry looked as if it was on the verge of defeat. The relentless patrolling, robust communication network, accurate weapons placement, and dedicated fire support led the 38th Cavalry Squadron's ability to overcome the overwhelming odds against the German *LXVII Corps*.

---

[280] CPT Jenter, C. M., "Prisoner of War Interrogation Report," January 19, 1945. in "After Action Report, 38th Cavalry Reconnaissance Squadron (Mechanized), Aug 44 thru April 45." n.d. Ike Skelton Combined Arms Research Library (CARL) Digital Library. 2011. World War II Operational Documents. May 16, 2011.

Chapter VII: Other Views

"What is history but a fable agreed upon?"
-Napoleon Bonaparte

Historians have "danced around the subject" over the years. Still, with more specific research, historians might be able to gain a greater understanding of the Ardennes Offensive and World War II if the Defense of Monschau is studied more. When researching the Defense of Monschau, a glaring void in the historiography is displayed. Historians briefly mention the Defense of Monschau by the 38th Cavalry Squadron in academic writings, ultimately glancing over the small but essential battle. An in-depth understanding of the 38th Cavalry Squadron's stand at Monschau adds to the understanding of how the Allies were able to hold their positions along the northern shoulder, thwarting the German advance on Antwerp. The Ardennes Offensive is arguably one of the most studied battles of the Second World War. An understanding of how the Defense of Monschau facilitated the Allies holding the northern shoulder, and eventually dismantling the Third Reich, will add to the significance of the Ardennes Offensive as a significant turning point in world history. Looking for the heroic stories of the 38th Cavalry and the actions that took place during the Defense of Monschau, historians quickly find that they must broaden the scope of their research to find any mention of Monschau.

Knowledge of the terrain adds a great contextual understanding of the Defense of Monschau. Historians have studied the terrain and the effects the Ardennes Forest had on the battlefield to gain an understanding of the fighting across the entire Ardennes Offensive front. The common consensus from many historians is that the terrain surrounding Monschau consists of several high ridges and steep hills. Trees cover the entire area, and in some places, the tree canopy is too thick for the sun to reach the ground floor.[281] This complex terrain has impacted military operations, and historians have varied on what specific piece or variable of terrain has impacted the battlefield most. Joseph Giarrusso argues that specific variables such as average rainfall affected how the Germans attacked through the Ardennes and Monschau area in World War I (1914) and World War II (1940).[282] Marvin Gordon argues that the perception military commanders had of the Ardennes region affected how the Germans attacked. Gordon points out that in 1940 French commanders believed the Ardennes region to be an area too difficult to traverse or attack, therefore explaining why the

---

[281] Bradbeer, Thomas G., "General Cota and the Battle of the Hurtgen Forest: A Failure of Battle Command?" *Army History,* no. 75 (2010); Giarrusso, Joseph Martin, "Against all odds: the story of the 106th Infantry Division in the Battle of the Bulge" (1998). *Master's Theses.* 1743; MacDonald, Charles B., *The Battle of the Hurtgen Forest,"* [1st Ed.] ed. Great Battles of History. (Philadelphia: Lippincott, 1963); Hull, Mike, "Slog Through the Hurtgen Forest," *Military History,* January 2018.

[282] Giarrusso, "Against all odds," 25-28.

French left the Ardennes region so lightly defended. He later states how the perception of the Ardennes Forest changed and, in 1944, was deliberately occupied by the Allies.[283]

The town of Monschau lies on the outskirts of the Hurtgen Forest, and to gain better apperception of the terrain surrounding Monschau, examining the Hurtgen Forest helps fill the gap of detailed information. Charles MacDonald analyzed the terrain, concluding that Monschau and its surroundings provided a tactical advantage to both the Allies and the Germans due to its high terrain. MacDonald centers this argument around the plateau-like clearings that provided great observation of the main roads for whoever occupied the plateau. The Allies had to position themselves in clearings to observe the roads from the plateau, which allowed the Germans to observe the Allies' location and strength.[284] Mike Hull argues that the high ridgelines and complex terrain were a disadvantage to both the Allies and Germans. Hull concludes that due to the terrain, and regardless of weather, air support would not have been practical.[285] Thomas Bradbeer is the only historian to give a specific piece of terrain that effected the fighting in the Hurtgen Forest and Ardennes region. Bradbeer argues that the Kall River is the most critical piece of terrain in the surrounding area. The Kall River played a significant role in

---

[283] Gordon, Marvin F., "Physiography and Military Perception The Case of Plan XVII, the Ardennes, Caporetto, and the Taebaek Split." *Army History*, no. 39 (1996): 21-22.

[284] MacDonald, *The Battle of the Hurtgen Forest,"* 39.

[285] Hull, "Slog Through the Hurtgen Forest," 39.

General Cota's defeat during the Battle of the Hurtgen Forest. The Kall River joins the Roer River east of Monschau and played a significant role during the Defense of Monschau. Bradbeer states the importance of both the Kall and Roer River but never expands on this thought.[286]

As historians began to look deeper into the Ardennes Offensive, one of the first questions they looked to answer was to identify the German operational goal for the Ardennes Offensive. Most historians agree that the German operational objective was the city of Antwerp. Hitler's tactical plan to get to Antwerp is agreed upon by historians. The German tactical plan for the Ardennes Offensive was an attack through the Ardennes Forrest, between Echternach and Monschau, with smaller objectives being to secure the bridgeheads over the Meuse River between Liege and Namur. The German plan was to have two main thrusts over a 45-mile front.[287] Commonly debated between historians and authors, is the reason why Antwerp was the operational objective. The port of Antwerp was facilitating the Allied flow of supplies across the European continent and the Allied lines. Hitler's specific objective for Antwerp was to seize the Port of Antwerp.[288] The

[286] Bradbeer, "General Cota and the Battle of the Hurtgen Forest," 24.

[287] Claflin, R.C., *"The Operational Art as Practiced by General George Patton, Jr. During the Battle of the Bulge"*, https://apps.dtic.mil/dtic/tr/fulltext/u2/a283522.pdf, 17 Jun 1994, 8; Nash, Douglas E., "KESTERNICH: The Battle That Saved the Bulge," *Army History*, no. 109 (2018).

[288] Claflin, R.C., *"The Operational Art as Practiced by General George Patton, Jr. During the Battle of the Bulge"*, 6;

Allied logistical network was their most significant vulnerability. Hitler believed that if he controlled Antwerp, he would sever US General Dwight D. Eisenhower's supply lines and demoralize the Allies. The control of Antwerp would also rejuvenate the Nazi U-boat campaign. Hitler previously utilized U-boats to take meteorological readings to identify when the weather would be best in their favor.[289] Combining arguments, historians and readers gain a greater understanding Antwerp had to a landlocked Germany.

Other historians have claimed that while Antwerp was Hitler's operational objective, Hitler believed the German control of Antwerp would facilitate a peace deal between the Allies and Germany.[290] Hanson Baldwin expounds on why Hitler wanted a peace deal with the Allies. Baldwin claims that Hitler launched the Ardennes Offensive to avoid major armed conflict along both the Nazi eastern and western fronts.[291] Hitler had reason to believe that an impending Soviet offensive would start in January 1945 that would require him to split his forces into two fronts, in the east against the Soviets, and in the west against the

---

Weinberg, Gerhard L., "German Plans for Victory, 1944-45," *Central European History* 26, no. 2 (1993): 221-223.

[289] Weinberg, "German Plans for Victory, 1944-45," 221-223.; Caddick-Adams, Peter, *Snow & Steel: The Battle of the Bulge, 1944-45*, (New York: Oxford University Press, 2017), 116.

[290] Baldwin, Hanson W., "America at War: The Winter Months." *Foreign Affairs* 23, no. 3 (1945); Claflin, *"The Operational Art as Practiced by General George Patton, Jr. During the Battle of the Bulge,"* 8;

[291] Baldwin, "America at War," 388.

US and British. Baldwin expounded in greater detail that a sub-objective for Germany seizing Antwerp was to desynchronize the Allied plan.[292] David Yelton agrees that Hitler's Ardennes Offensive was to result in a peace treaty. However, the establishment of the German *Volkssturm*[293] was Hitler's solution to achieving conditions for a peace treaty.[294] Yelton presents different problems that Germany faced late in 1944 till the end of the war and how the *Volkssturm* was the solution. Yelton also describes Hitler's dilemma in fighting a war on two fronts, a claim that re-enforces Hanson Baldwin's argument.[295]

Heinrich Schwendemann and Gerhard Weinberg have examined reasons for why Hitler conducted such a major offensive operation in the late stages of World War II. Schwendemann focuses on Albert Speer and concludes, through the written correspondence between Hitler and Speer, that Speer convinced Hitler that he could increase armament for the German Army as late as January 1945.[296] Gerhard Weinberg provided the counter-argument by stating that even as other European Axis powers

---

[292] Ibid., 390.

[293] The Volkssturm was a national militia established by the Nazi Party consisting of males that were not already serving in a military unit.

[294] Yelton, David K., "Ein Volk Steht Auf": The German Volkssturm and Nazi Strategy, 1944-45." *The Journal of Military History* 64, no. 4 (2000): 1063-1064, 1076.

[295] Baldwin, "America at War," 338; Yelton, "Ein Volk Steht Auf," 1064-1065.

[296] Schwendemann, Heinrich, "Drastic Measures to Defend the Reich at the Order and the Rhine…: A Forgotten Memorandum of Albert Speer of 18 March 1945." *Journal of Contemporary History* Vol. 38, No. 4 (2003): 598.

sought peace negotiations with the Allies, German still believed it was strategically able to overpower the Allies.[297]

Historians have also viewed Hitler's relationship with his subordinate leaders as an area of academic study. Historians agree that Hitler did not trust his subordinates, which created tensions throughout the Third Reich.[298] Peter Caddick-Adams concludes that in late 1944 the German military resembled the armies of World War I, who lacked supplies and resources. The state of the German Army contributed to Hitler's trust issues with his subordinates. Danny Parker interviews several high-ranking German Generals and displays the disconnect they had with Hitler due to his inability to trust his subordinates. Each officer interviewed provides an overview on the desperate state of the German Army before the Ardennes Offensive began. They also provide not only their personal views of Hitler and his plan for the Ardennes Offensive but also what they believe was the tactical plan needed to achieve victory and the seizure of Antwerp.

Similarly, Ralph Mitchell observes the disconnect between Hitler and his generals, summarizing that Hitler's staff did not fully understand his intentions

---

[297] Weinberg, "German Plans for Victory, 1944-45," 215.

[298] Caddick-Adams, Peter, *Snow & Steel: The Battle of the Bulge, 1944-45*, (New York: Oxford University Press, 2017); Parker, Danny S., *Hitler's Ardennes Offensive: The German View of the Battle of the Bulge,* (New York: Skyhorse Publishing, 2016); Mitchell, Ralph M., "The 101st Airborne Division's Defense of Bastogne." *Combat Studies Institute,* US Army Command & General Staff College, (1986).

for the Ardennes Offensive. Hitler's staff concluded that the capture of Bastogne would not be necessary, but that Bastogne only needed to be encircled. The German staff was more worried about the timeline for the Ardennes Offensive as they were also concerned with the impending Russian offensive on the Eastern front.[299]

Similarly, historians have examined the Allied response to the Ardennes Offensive and argue that different specific battles within the Ardennes Offensive became the turning point for the Allies. Many historians differ on the specifics surrounding a battle resulting in historians' overall arguments rarely being the same. Many historians determine that the US 101st Airborne Divisions defense at Bastogne was the turning point for the Allies.[300] John McManus argues that the 101st Airborne Division would not have been successful in reaching Bastogne in time had the US 28th Infantry Division, the Combat Command Reserve of the US 9th Armored Division, and the Combat Command B of the US 10th Armored Division delayed the Germans.[301] McManus continues by displaying that by December 25th, 1944, Bastogne lost its importance to the Germans as they became entrenched in a battle of attrition. Ralph Mitchell concludes that the flexibility of

---

[299] Mitchell, "The 101st Airborne Division's Defense of Bastogne," 3.

[300] McManus, John C., *Alamo in the Ardennes: The Untold Story of the American Soldiers Who Made the Defense of Bastogne Possible*, (New York: NAL Caliber, 2008) xiii; Mitchell, Ralph M., "The 101st Airborne Division's Defense of Bastogne." *Combat Studies Institute,* US Army Command & General Staff College, (1986).

[301] McManus, *Alamo in the Ardennes,* xiii.

the 101st Airborne Division to organizationally reconfigure for sustained operations resulted in their victory at Bastogne.[302] He states that early in the planning process, the Germans identified that Bastogne held the vital crossroads that would be essential to maintaining lines of communications. Hitler specifically ordered the capture of Bastogne.[303] In the early stages of the Ardennes Offensive, Allied leaders also identified Bastogne as being vital to the Germans and that if the Allies could hold Bastogne, they could interrupt the German communication lines.[304] The backbone of Mitchell's argument is the timeline that occurred versus the planned timeline.

Historians have provided a counterargument to McManus and Mitchell by concluding that the Defense of St. Vith as being the turning point for the Allies.[305] Frank Andrews comes to his conclusion by explaining that the German defeat at St. Vith was their first major defeat of the Ardennes Offensive and disrupted and desynchronized the German tactical plan.[306] Joseph Giarrusso agrees with Andrews that

[302] Mitchell, "The 101st Airborne Division's Defense of Bastogne," 1.

[303] Mitchell, "The 101st Airborne Division's Defense of Bastogne," 3.

[304] Mitchell, "The 101st Airborne Division's Defense of Bastogne," 4.

[305] Andrews, Frank L., *The Defense of St. Vith in the Battle of the Ardennes, December, 1944* (MA Thesis, Department of American Civilization, New York University, 1964); Giarrusso, Joseph Martin, "Against all odds: the story of the 106th Infantry Division in the Battle of the Bulge" (1998). *Master's Theses.* 1743.

[306] Andrews, *The Defense of St. Vith in the Battle of the Ardennes, December,* ii.

the Defense of St. Vith was the turning point for the Allies, but that the US 106th Infantry Division, who participated in the Defense of St. Vith, threw off the timing of the German *Fifth Panzer Army* long enough for the Allies to recover and counterattack.[307] Giarrusso supports his argument by explaining how the US 106th Infantry Division faced a more concentrated amount of Germans and took more casualties than any other division in World War II, resulting in them becoming decimated and destroyed during the Ardennes Offensive.[308]

Historians have also demonstrated the different tensions among the Allied Commanders. The largest area of contention between Allied commanders was between US General George S. Patton, General Eisenhower, and other Allied Generals.[309] Franklin Gurley displays how each Allied commander believed they were in the best position to seize Berlin. General Eisenhower placed British Field Marshall Bernard Montgomery (commander of the 21st Army Group) in command of the north side of the "bulge," and took reserve units from US General Jacob L. Devers (commander of the 6th Army Group) and US General

---

[307] Andrews, *The Defense of St. Vith in the Battle of the Ardennes, December,* 2-3.

[308] Giarrusso, "Against all odds," 2.

[309] Claflin, "The Operational Art as Practiced by General George Patton, Jr. During the Battle of the Bulge", 2; Gurley, Franklin Louis. *"Policy Versus Strategy: The Defense of Strasbourg in Winter 1944-1945." The Journal of Military History* 58, no. 3 (1994): 482, 485-486; Caddick-Adams, *Snow & Steel: The Battle of the Bulge, 1944-45*, 419-420; D'Este, Carlos, "Patton's Finest Hour," *Mhq: The Quarterly Journal of Military History* 13 (3) (2001).

Omar Bradley (commander of the 12th Army Group). General Eisenhower ordered General Patton (commander of the 3rd Army Group) to move north and relieve pressure in the Ardennes Forest.[310] Gurley expertly explains the shuffling of units General Eisenhower conducted in an attempt to counter the German attack, but that this shuffling resulted in many Generals having discord with General Patton and General Eisenhower. Carlos D'Este expounds on Gurley's thesis by displaying the tensions between Allied commanders, centered around General Patton. General Eisenhower continually questioned General Patton's leadership throughout the war.[311] Other Allied generals and officers on General Patton's staff questioned his ability to move the 3rd Army Group in time to assist the 1st Army Group and the 101st Airborne Division at Bastogne.[312]

Continuing along with the trend of analyzing the Allied response to the Ardennes Offensive, historians have examined how the Allies were in a position to allow the German offensive. Historians have concluded that the Allied command relied upon the intelligence community, ULTRA, to provide accurate information on Germans activity resulting in known weakened Allied positions.[313] Drew Middleton

---

[310] Gurley, Franklin Louis. "Policy Versus Strategy: The Defense of Strasbourg in Winter 1944-1945." *The Journal of Military History* 58, no. 3 (1994): 482, 485-486.

[311] D'Este, "Patton's Finest Hour," 19.

[312] D'Este, "Patton's Finest Hour," 20.

[313] Middleton, Drew, "The Battle that Sealed Germany's Fate." *The New York Times*, December 16, 1984, sec. 6; Baldwin, "America at War," 389; Deming, Dennis C., Army

provides evidence that senior Allied commanders knew of the weak Allied formations along the Ardennes region but became complacent in relying on ULTRA and believed that Germany was unable to mount a formidable attack. General Bradly was in command of the Ardennes region and knew of the weakened defensive positions but claimed that the Germans would not attack through the Ardennes. US General Troy H. Middleton, commander of the US VIII Corps, reminded General Bradley that the Germans had a history of attacking through the Ardennes region and not to overestimate the Germans.[314] Drew Middleton concludes that ULTRA knew of a pending German attack but failed to thoroughly understand the time and place of the attack, as well as Hitler's operational goal.[315] Carlos D'Este provides a different argument on the Allied use and trust of ULTRA. He states that the 3rd Army Group intelligence officer knew of the German build-up of infantry and armored divisions, ammunition, and fuel depots across the Ardennes region before the German attack.[316]

When historians have mentioned the Defense of

War College (U.S.) 1989. AD-A 207 997, Carlisle Barracks, Pa. : U.S. Army War College, http://www.dtic.mil/dtic/tr/fulltext/u2/a207997.pdf "7 March 1989." USAWC Military Studies Program paper; Student papers, ii, 34 p.; 28 cm; ii; MacDonald, Charles B., *A Time For Trumpets,* (New York: Morrow, 1985).

[314] Middleton, "The Battle that Sealed Germany's Fate," 2; MacDonald, *A Time For Trumpets,* 39-80.

[315] Middleton, "The Battle that Sealed Germany's Fate," 7.

[316] D'Este, "Patton's Finest Hour," 17.

Monschau in academic work, they heavily focus on the German plan at Monschau, looking for reasons for their failed attack. The consensus is that the German *LXVII Corp* failed to mass its combat power at Monschau, resulting in the 38th Cavalry's ability to defend the town successfully.[317] John Eisenhower describes the German plan along the northern shoulder by stating that the German *LXVII Corps, 246th*, and *322nd Volksgrenadier Divisions* attacked Monschau. Once the Volksgrenadier Divisions were successful at Monschau, the *XLVII Corps* and the *1st SS Panzer Corps* were to push northwest and protect the northern flank of the Ardennes Offensive.[318] Douglas Nash expounds on why the German plan failed along the northern shoulder. Nash states that German *General der Infanterie Otto Hitzfeld[319]*, commander of the *LXVII Corps*, failed to penetrate the Allied lines to the town of Eupen, resulting in the *LXVII Corps'* inability to protect the northern flank of the German *6th Panzer Army*.[320] Roger Cirillo provides the counterargument by stating that the *LXVII Corps* was to bypass Monschau altogether. Cirillo claims that this bypass would have

---

[317] Reynolds, Michael Frank, *"The Devil's Adjutant: Jochen Peiper, Panzer Leader,"* (New York: Sarpedon, 1995); Elstob, Peter, *Hitler's Last Offensive*, (London: Secker and Warburg, 1971) 192-193; Nash, Douglas E., "KESTERNICH: The Battle That Saved the Bulge," *Army History*, no. 109 (2018).

[318] Eisenhower, John S. D., *The Bitter Woods: The Dramatic Story of Hitler's Surprise Ardennes Offensive*, (London: Robert Hale, 1969) 158.

[319] At the time of the Ardennes Offensive, Otto Hitzfeld was a Generalleutnant. Roughly translated to General Lieutenant.

[320] Nash, "KESTERNICH: The Battle That Saved the Bulge," 48.

allowed the *277th* and *326th Volksgrenadier Divisions* to block the main roads, allowing the German *1st SS Panzer Corps* to move northwest and protect the flank of the German *5th Panzer Army.*[321]   Cirillo's statement contradicts all previous academic arguments to the tactical advantage of Monschau by implying that Monschau held no strategic importance to the Germans.

When it comes to the 38th Cavalry's stand at Monschau, few historians provide reasons for the 38th Cavalry's success. Charles MacDonald claims that the direct support of the 405th Field Artillery Group was the vital "piece" to the defense of Monschau and the neighboring town Mutzenich.[322]   William C.C. Cavanagh's also provides his opinion on what made the 38th Cavalry's defense at Monschau successful. He concludes that the 38th Cavalry was well established in Monschau before the German attack.[323]

During the Ardennes Offensive, why did the Allies' "northern shoulder" hold its position in Monschau and not fall to the German *LXVII Corps*? The 38th Cavalry Squadron correctly anticipated German battle plans in the area of Monschau by establishing an effective communication network, an aggressive patrol schedule, weapon placement, and field artillery support.

---

[321] Cirillo, Roger, *Ardennes-Alsace*, (Washington, D.C.: U.S. Army Center of Military History, 2019) 13-14.

[322] MacDonald, *A Time For Trumpets*, 163-167.

[323] Cavanagh, William C. C., and Karl Cavanagh, *A Tour of the Bulge Battlefields,"* (Barnsley: Pen & Sword Military, 2015) 27.

Bibliography

Primary Sources

1LT Allen, Albert C., "Missions fired by Troop E, 38th Cav Rcn Sq (Mecz) from 160600A December 1944 to 170600A December 1944," in "After Action Report, 38th Cavalry Reconnaissance Squadron (Mechanized), Aug 44 thru April 45." n.d. Ike Skelton Combined Arms Research Library (CARL) Digital Library. 2011. World War II Operational Documents. May 16, 2011. http://cgsc.cdmhost.com/cdm/ref/collection/p4013coll8/i d/3729.

Tec 5 Anderson, Allen J., "Report of Tec 5 Allen J. Anderson, Troop C, 38th Cav Rcn Sq (Mecz)," in "After Action Report, 38th Cavalry Reconnaissance Squadron (Mechanized), Aug 44 thru April 45." n.d. Ike Skelton Combined Arms Research Library (CARL) Digital Library. 2011. World War II Operational Documents. May 16, 2011.
http://cgsc.cdmhost.com/cdm/ref/collection/p4013coll 8/id/3729.

S/SGT Bielicki, Bernard C., "Report of Staff Sergeant Bernard C. Bielicki, Platoon Sergeant, 2nd Platoon, Company F, 38th CAV RCN SQ (MECZ)," December 16, 1944. in "After Action Report, 38th Cavalry Reconnaissance Squadron (Mechanized), Aug 44 thru April 45." n.d. Ike Skelton Combined Arms Research Library (CARL) Digital Library. 2011. World War II Operational Documents. May 16, 2011.

http://cgsc.cdmhost.com/cdm/ref/collection/p4013coll8/id/3729.

S/SGT Bielicki, Bernard C.,"Affidavit," January 18, 1945. in "After Action Report, 38th Cavalry Reconnaissance Squadron (Mechanized), Aug 44 thru April 45." n.d. Ike Skelton Combined Arms Research Library (CARL) Digital Library. 2011. World War II Operational Documents. May 16, 2011.
http://cgsc.cdmhost.com/cdm/ref/collection/p4013coll8/id/3729.

CPL Brown, Walter E., "Affidavit," January 24, 1945. in "After Action Report, 38th Cavalry Reconnaissance Squadron (Mechanized), Aug 44 thru April 45." n.d. Ike Skelton Combined Arms Research Library (CARL) Digital Library. 2011. World War II Operational Documents. May 16, 2011.
http://cgsc.cdmhost.com/cdm/ref/collection/p4013coll8/id/3729.

PVT Carpenter, Aaron B., "Affidavit," January 24, 1945. in "After Action Report, 38th Cavalry Reconnaissance Squadron (Mechanized), Aug 44 thru April 45." n.d. Ike Skelton Combined Arms Research Library (CARL) Digital Library. 2011. World War II Operational Documents. May 16, 2011.
http://cgsc.cdmhost.com/cdm/ref/collection/p4013coll8/id/3729.

1LT Coleman, Raphail V., "Report of 1st LT Raphail V. Coleman, Platoon Leader, 3rd Platoon, Troop C, 38 Cav. Rcn. Sq.," December 16-17, 1944. in "After Action

Report, 38th Cavalry Reconnaissance Squadron (Mechanized), Aug 44 thru April 45." n.d. Ike Skelton Combined Arms Research Library (CARL) Digital Library. 2011. World War II Operational Documents. May 16, 2011.

http://cgsc.cdmhost.com/cdm/ref/collection/p4013coll 8/id/3729.

1LT Comfort, James A., "Certificate," January 22, 1945. in "After Action Report, 38th Cavalry Reconnaissance Squadron (Mechanized), Aug 44 thru April 45." n.d. Ike Skelton Combined Arms Research Library (CARL) Digital Library. 2011. World War II Operational Documents. May 16, 2011.

http://cgsc.cdmhost.com/cdm/ref/collection/p4013coll 8/id/3729.

1LT Cullinan, Robert J., "Report of 1st LT. Robert J. Cullinan 1032424 Platoon Leader, 3rd Platoon, Company F, 38th CAV RCN SQ," in "After Action Report, 38th Cavalry Reconnaissance Squadron (Mechanized), Aug 44 thru April 45." n.d. Ike Skelton Combined Arms Research Library (CARL) Digital Library. 2011. World War II Operational Documents. May 16, 2011. http://cgsc.cdmhost.com/cdm/ref/collection/p4013coll8/i d/3729.

1LT Cullinan, Robert J., "Certificate," January 18, 1945. in "After Action Report, 38th Cavalry Reconnaissance Squadron (Mechanized), Aug 44 thru April 45." n.d. Ike Skelton Combined Arms Research Library (CARL) Digital Library. 2011. World War II Operational Documents. May 16, 2011.

http://cgsc.cdmhost.com/cdm/ref/collection/p4013coll
8/id/3729.

MAJ Fingerhut, R. V., "Fires: Extract," in "After
Action Report, 38th Cavalry Reconnaissance Squadron
(Mechanized), Aug 44 thru April 45." n.d. Ike Skelton
Combined Arms Research Library (CARL) Digital
Library. 2011. World War II Operational Documents.
May 16, 2011.
http://cgsc.cdmhost.com/cdm/ref/collection/p4013coll
8/id/3729.

S/SGT Fisher, William F., "Report of S/SGT William
F. Fisher, 35438173, Forward Observer, Troop B, 38th
Cav Rcn Sq," in "After Action Report, 38th Cavalry
Reconnaissance Squadron (Mechanized), Aug 44 thru
April 45." n.d. Ike Skelton Combined Arms Research
Library (CARL) Digital Library. 2011. World War II
Operational Documents. May 16, 2011.
http://cgsc.cdmhost.com/cdm/ref/collection/p4013coll
8/id/3729.

CPT Frink, George R., "S-2 Estimate of Enemy
Forces to Immediate Front of 38th Cav on 17 December
1944, as result of PW Interrogation," January 11, 1945. in
"After Action Report, 38th Cavalry Reconnaissance
Squadron (Mechanized), Aug 44 thru April 45." n.d. Ike
Skelton Combined Arms Research Library (CARL)
Digital Library. 2011. World War II Operational
Documents. May 16, 2011.
http://cgsc.cdmhost.com/cdm/ref/collection/p4013coll
8/id/3729.

CPT Frink, George R., Report Title Unreadable, in

"After Action Report, 38th Cavalry Reconnaissance Squadron (Mechanized), Aug 44 thru April 45." n.d. Ike Skelton Combined Arms Research Library (CARL) Digital Library. 2011. World War II Operational Documents. May 16, 2011.

http://cgsc.cdmhost.com/cdm/ref/collection/p4013coll 8/id/3729.

CPT Frink, George R., "Report of Captain George R. Frink S-2, 38th CAV. RCN. SQ (MECZ) of Dead Germans Reported by Troop C, 38th CAV. RCN. SQ. (MECZ)," in "After Action Report, 38th Cavalry Reconnaissance Squadron (Mechanized), Aug 44 thru April 45." n.d. Ike Skelton Combined Arms Research Library (CARL) Digital Library. 2011. World War II Operational Documents. May 16, 2011.

http://cgsc.cdmhost.com/cdm/ref/collection/p4013coll 8/id/3729.

TEC/5 Gier, Joseph C., "Report of Joseph C. Gier 32583371, 3rd Platoon, Company F, 38th CAV RCN SQ (MECZ)," December 17, 1944. in "After Action Report, 38th Cavalry Reconnaissance Squadron (Mechanized), Aug 44 thru April 45." n.d. Ike Skelton Combined Arms Research Library (CARL) Digital Library. 2011. World War II Operational Documents. May 16, 2011.

http://cgsc.cdmhost.com/cdm/ref/collection/p4013coll 8/id/3729.

CPT Goetcheus, Robert A., "Military Government Periodic Report No. 78" in "After Action Report, 38th Cavalry Reconnaissance Squadron (Mechanized), Aug 44 thru April 45." n.d. Ike Skelton Combined Arms

Research Library (CARL) Digital Library. 2011. World War II Operational Documents. May 16, 2011.

http://cgsc.cdmhost.com/cdm/ref/collection/p4013coll 8/id/3729.

2LT Harf, Arthur, "Consolidated Interrogated Report of P/W's captured 16-18 Dec 44," January 25, 1945. in "After Action Report, 38th Cavalry Reconnaissance Squadron (Mechanized), Aug 44 thru April 45." n.d. Ike Skelton Combined Arms Research Library (CARL) Digital Library. 2011. World War II Operational Documents. May 16, 2011.

http://cgsc.cdmhost.com/cdm/ref/collection/p4013coll 8/id/3729.

CPT Jenter, C. M., "Prisoner of War Interrogation Report," January 19, 1945. in "After Action Report, 38th Cavalry Reconnaissance Squadron (Mechanized), Aug 44 thru April 45." n.d. Ike Skelton Combined Arms Research Library (CARL) Digital Library. 2011. World War II Operational Documents. May 16, 2011.

http://cgsc.cdmhost.com/cdm/ref/collection/p4013coll 8/id/3729.

2LT Ketz, Howard E., "Report of 2nd LT Ketz, Platoon Leader, 1st Platoon, Company F," December 17, 1944. in "After Action Report, 38th Cavalry Reconnaissance Squadron (Mechanized), Aug 44 thru April 45." n.d. Ike Skelton Combined Arms Research Library (CARL) Digital Library. 2011. World War II Operational Documents. May 16, 2011.

http://cgsc.cdmhost.com/cdm/ref/collection/p4013coll 8/id/3729.

2LT Ketz, Howard E., "Certificate," December 17, 1944. in "After Action Report, 38th Cavalry Reconnaissance Squadron (Mechanized), Aug 44 thru April 45." n.d. Ike Skelton Combined Arms Research Library (CARL) Digital Library. 2011. World War II Operational Documents. May 16, 2011.
http://cgsc.cdmhost.com/cdm/ref/collection/p4013coll 8/id/3729.

CPL Leone, n.d. Raymond J., "In Front of the Front-Line: WWII stories written by a Scout from the 38th Cavalry Reconnaissance Squadron Mechanized." NJ Cavalry and Armor Association. Accessed January 19, 2020.
http://njcavalryandarmorassociation.org/history.html

S/SGT Lindquist, Kenneth C., "Report of Staff Sergeant Kenneth C. Lindquist, Platoon Sergeant, 3rd Platoon, Company F, 38th CAV RCN SQ (MECZ)" December 17, 1944. in "After Action Report, 38th Cavalry Reconnaissance Squadron (Mechanized), Aug 44 thru April 45." n.d. Ike Skelton Combined Arms Research Library (CARL) Digital Library. 2011. World War II Operational Documents. May 16, 2011.
http://cgsc.cdmhost.com/cdm/ref/collection/p4013coll 8/id/3729.

S/SGT Lindquist, Kenneth C., "Affidavit," January 18, 1945. in "After Action Report, 38th Cavalry Reconnaissance Squadron (Mechanized), Aug 44 thru April 45." n.d. Ike Skelton Combined Arms Research Library (CARL) Digital Library. 2011. World War II

Operational Documents. May 16, 2011.
http://cgsc.cdmhost.com/cdm/ref/collection/p4013coll
8/id/3729.

SGT Messano, Martin P., "Affidavit." in "After Action
Report, 38th Cavalry Reconnaissance Squadron
(Mechanized), Aug 44 thru April 45." n.d. Ike Skelton
Combined Arms Research Library (CARL) Digital
Library. 2011. World War II Operational Documents.
May 16, 2011.
http://cgsc.cdmhost.com/cdm/ref/collection/p4013coll
8/id/3729.

Tec 5 Misch, Fred T., "Affidavit," January 24, 1945. in
"After Action Report, 38th Cavalry Reconnaissance
Squadron (Mechanized), Aug 44 thru April 45." n.d. Ike
Skelton Combined Arms Research Library (CARL)
Digital Library. 2011. World War II Operational
Documents. May 16, 2011.
http://cgsc.cdmhost.com/cdm/ref/collection/p4013coll
8/id/3729.

SGT Okenhan, Charles E., "Affidavit," January 24,
1945. in "After Action Report, 38th Cavalry
Reconnaissance Squadron (Mechanized), Aug 44 thru
April 45." n.d. Ike Skelton Combined Arms Research
Library (CARL) Digital Library. 2011. World War II
Operational Documents. May 16, 2011.
http://cgsc.cdmhost.com/cdm/ref/collection/p4013coll
8/id/3729.

"Orgn and Equipment of Mechanized Cav Units." n.d.
Ike Skelton Combined Arms Research Library (CARL)

Digital Library. Accessed January 19, 2020. https://cgsc.contentdm.oclc.org/cdm/ref/collection/p1242 01col2/id/135

1LT O'Brien, James J., "Report of 1st LT James J. O'Brien, Platoon Leader, 1st Platoon, Tr C," in "After Action Report, 38th Cavalry Reconnaissance Squadron (Mechanized), Aug 44 thru April 45." n.d. Ike Skelton Combined Arms Research Library (CARL) Digital Library. 2011. World War II Operational Documents. May 16, 2011. http://cgsc.cdmhost.com/cdm/ref/collection/p4013coll8/i d/3729.

LTC O'Brien, Robert E., "After Action Report, 38th Cavalry Reconnaissance Squadron (Mechanized), Aug 44 thru April 45." n.d. Ike Skelton Combined Arms Research Library (CARL) Digital Library. 2011. World War II Operational Documents. May 16, 2011.
http://cgsc.cdmhost.com/cdm/ref/collection/p4013coll 8/id/3729.

LTC O'Brien, Robert E., "Operations Map #2," in "After Action Report, 38th Cavalry Reconnaissance Squadron (Mechanized), Aug 44 thru April 45." n.d. Ike Skelton Combined Arms Research Library (CARL) Digital Library. 2011. World War II Operational Documents. May 16, 2011.
http://cgsc.cdmhost.com/cdm/ref/collection/p4013coll 8/id/3729.

PFC Pirera, Joseph B., "Affidavit," in "After Action Report, 38th Cavalry Reconnaissance Squadron

(Mechanized), Aug 44 thru April 45." n.d. Ike Skelton Combined Arms Research Library (CARL) Digital Library. 2011. World War II Operational Documents. May 16, 2011.
http://cgsc.cdmhost.com/cdm/ref/collection/p4013coll 8/id/3729.

PFC Riegel, Bernard F., "Affidavit," January 24, 1945. in "After Action Report, 38th Cavalry Reconnaissance Squadron (Mechanized), Aug 44 thru April 45." n.d. Ike Skelton Combined Arms Research Library (CARL) Digital Library. 2011. World War II Operational Documents. May 16, 2011.
http://cgsc.cdmhost.com/cdm/ref/collection/p4013coll 8/id/3729.

CPT Rogers, Elmer L., "Report of Capitan Elmer L. Rogers, Commanding Officer, Troop C, 38th CAV RCN SQ (MECZ)," in "After Action Report, 38th Cavalry Reconnaissance Squadron (Mechanized), Aug 44 thru April 45." n.d. Ike Skelton Combined Arms Research Library (CARL) Digital Library. 2011. World War II Operational Documents. May 16, 2011.
http://cgsc.cdmhost.com/cdm/ref/collection/p4013coll 8/id/3729.

MAJ Rousek, Charles E. n.d., "A Short History of the 38th Cavalry Reconnaissance Squadron (Mechanized)." NJ Cavalry and Armor Association. Accessed January 19, 2020.
http://njcavalryandarmorassociation.org/history.html
MAJ Rousek, Charles E., "Defense of Monschau." June 23, 2012.

http://battleofthebulgememories.be/stories26/us-army25/648-defense-of-monschau.html

1LT Ross, Wesley, "The Bulge: Per the 146th Engineer Combat Bn." February 3, 2014.
http://battleofthebulgememories.be/stories26/us-army25/831-the-bulge-per-the-146th-engineer-combat-bn.html.

MAJ Russen, David M. n.d., "Combat History, 102nd Cavalry Reconnaissance Squadron (Mecz), World War II." NJ Cavalry and Armor Association. Accessed January 19, 2020.
http://njcavalryandarmorassociation.org/history.html

CPT Sain, Joseph R., "Report of Captain Joseph R. Sain 0-1030828, Troop Commander, Troop B, 38th CAV RCN SQ," December 16-18, 1944. in "After Action Report, 38th Cavalry Reconnaissance Squadron (Mechanized), Aug 44 thru April 45." n.d. Ike Skelton Combined Arms Research Library (CARL) Digital Library. 2011. World War II Operational Documents. May 16, 2011.
http://cgsc.cdmhost.com/cdm/ref/collection/p4013coll8/id/3729.

2LT Shehab, Alfred H.M., "Extract of Statement of LT. Alfred H.M. Shehab in Recommendation of Award for Sergeant Florantius Becker," in "After Action Report, 38th Cavalry Reconnaissance Squadron (Mechanized), Aug 44 thru April 45." n.d. Ike Skelton Combined Arms Research Library (CARL) Digital Library. 2011. World War II Operational Documents. May 16, 2011.

http://cgsc.cdmhost.com/cdm/ref/collection/p4013coll
8/id/3729.

LTC (R) Shehab, Alfred H. M. n.d., "Cavalry On The
Shoulder: The 38th CRS and the Defense of Monschau."
NJ Cavalry and Armor Association. Accessed January
19, 2020.
http://njcavalryandarmorassociation.org/history.html

LTC (R) Shehab, Alfred H. M., "Defense of
Monschau by the 38th Cavalry Squadron." August 29,
2019.
http://battleofthebulgememories.be/stories26/us-
army25/953-defense-of-monschau-by-the-38th-cavalry-
squadron.html

T/4 Straigis, Anthony F., "Affidavit," January 9, 1945.
in "After Action Report, 38th Cavalry Reconnaissance
Squadron (Mechanized), Aug 44 thru April 45." n.d. Ike
Skelton Combined Arms Research Library (CARL)
Digital Library. 2011. World War II Operational
Documents. May 16, 2011.
http://cgsc.cdmhost.com/cdm/ref/collection/p4013coll
8/id/3729.

Tec. 4 Taylor, Russell F., Russell Taylor to Mary
Taylor, Salt Lake City, UT, November 1942-March 1945.

"Unit History, 38th Mechanized Cavalry
Reconnaissance Squadron, 9604 thru 9665." n.d. Ike
Skelton Combined Arms Research Library (CARL)
Digital Library. 2011.
World War II Operational Documents. May 27, 2011.

http://cgsc.cdmhost.com/cdm/ref/collection/p4013coll
8/id/3703

Colonel-Lt. Freiherr Von Der Heydte to The
Commanding Officer of the Military Government at
Monschau, December 22, 1944, in "After Action Report,
38th Cavalry Reconnaissance Squadron (Mechanized),
Aug 44 thru April 45." n.d. Ike Skelton Combined Arms
Research Library (CARL) Digital Library. 2011. World
War II Operational Documents. May 16, 2011.
http://cgsc.cdmhost.com/cdm/ref/collection/p4013coll
8/id/3729.

War Department, "FM 2-30 1943 (OBSOLETE):
Cavalry Field Manual, Cavalry Mechanized
Reconnaissance Squadron." n.d. Ike Skelton Combined
Arms Research Library (CARL) Digital Library. 2010.
Obsolete Military Manuals. December 16, 2010.
http://cdm16040.contentdm.oclc.org/cdm/singleitem/coll
ection/p4013coll9/id/709/rec/4.

War Department, "FM 100-5 1944 (OBSOLETE):
Field Service Regulations: Operations." n.d. Ike Skelton
Combined Arms Research Library (CARL).

MAJ Way, David W., "Certificate," January 21, 1945.
in "After Action Report, 38th Cavalry Reconnaissance
Squadron (Mechanized), Aug 44 thru April 45." n.d. Ike
Skelton Combined Arms Research Library (CARL)
Digital Library. 2011. World War II Operational
Documents. May 16, 2011.
http://cgsc.cdmhost.com/cdm/ref/collection/p4013coll
8/id/3729.

SGT West, Charles R., "Report of Sergeant Charles E. West 39127650, Platoon Sergeant, 2nd Platoon, Troop C, 38th CAV RCN SQ (MECZ)," December 16, 1944. in "After Action Report, 38th Cavalry Reconnaissance Squadron (Mechanized), Aug 44 thru April 45." n.d. Ike Skelton Combined Arms Research Library (CARL) Digital Library. 2011. World War II Operational Documents. May 16, 2011.
http://cgsc.cdmhost.com/cdm/ref/collection/p4013coll 8/id/3729.

2LT Yontz, W. J., "Report of 1st LT. W. J. Yontz, Platoon Leader, 2nd Platoon, Troop B, Action of 17 December 1944," in "After Action Report, 38th Cavalry Reconnaissance Squadron (Mechanized), Aug 44 thru April 45." n.d. Ike Skelton Combined Arms Research Library (CARL) Digital Library. 2011. World War II Operational Documents. May 16, 2011.
http://cgsc.cdmhost.com/cdm/ref/collection/p4013coll 8/id/3729.

S/SGT Zudkoff, Walter, "Report of S/SGT Walter (NMI) Zudkoff 12020660, Forward Observer, Troop E, 38th CAV RCN SQ (MECZ)," in "After Action Report, 38th Cavalry Reconnaissance Squadron (Mechanized), Aug 44 thru April 45." n.d. Ike Skelton Combined Arms Research Library (CARL) Digital Library. 2011. World War II Operational Documents. May 16, 2011.
http://cgsc.cdmhost.com/cdm/ref/collection/p4013coll 8/id/3729.

Secondary Sources

Caddick-Adams, Peter, *Snow & Steel: The Battle of the Bulge, 1944-45*, (New York: Oxford University Press, 2017).

Cavanagh, William C. C. and Karl Cavanagh, *A Tour of the Bulge Battlefields*, (Barnsley: Pen & Sword Military, 2015).

Cirillo, Roger, *Ardennes-Alsace*, (Washington, D.C.: U.S. Army Center of Military History, 2019).

Dupuy, Trevor N., David L. Bongard, and Richard C. Anderson, *Hitler's Last Gamble: The Battle of the Bulge, December 1944-January 1945*, (New York: Harper Perennial, 1995).

Eisenhower, John S. D., *The Bitter Woods: The Dramatic Story of Hitler's Surprise Ardenne Offensive*, (London: Robert Hale, 1969).

Elstob, Peter, *Hitler's Last Offensive*, (London: Secker and Warburg, 1971).

MacDonald, Charles B., *The Battle of the Hurtgen Forest*, [1st Ed.] ed. Great Battles of History. (Philadelphia: Lippincott, 1963).

MacDonald, Charles B., *A Time For Trumpets*, (New York: Morrow, 1985).

McManus, John C., *Alamo in the Ardennes: The*

Untold Story of the American Soldiers Who Made the Defense of Bastogne Possible, (New York: NAL Caliber, 2008).

Parker, Danny S., *Hitler's Ardennes Offensive: The German View of the Battle of the Bulge*, (London: Frontline Books, 2016).

Quarrie, Bruce, *The Ardennes Offensive: VI Panzer Armee: Northern Sector*, (Oxford: Osprey, 1999).

Reynolds, Michael Frank, *The Devil's Adjutant: Jochen Peiper, Panzer Leader*, (New York: Sarpedon, 1995).

Articles

Andrews, Frank L., The Defense of St. Vith in the Battle of the Ardennes, December, 1944 (MA Thesis, Department of American Civilization, New York University, 1964).

Baldwin, Hanson W., "America at War: The Winter Months." *Foreign Affairs* 23, no. 3 (1945): 388-405. doi:10.2307/20029905.

Bradbeer, Thomas G., "General Cota and the Battle of the Hurtgen Forest: A Failure of Battle Command?" *Army History*, no. 75 (2010): 18-41.
www.jstor.org/stable/26298911.

Claflin, R. C., "The Operational Art as Practiced by General George Patton, Jr. During the Battle of the Bulge",
https://apps.dtic.mil/dtic/tr/fulltext/u2/a283522.pdf, 17 Jun 1994.

Deming, Dennis C., Army War College (U.S.) 1989. AD-A 207 997, Carlisle Barracks, Pa.: U.S. Army War College,
http://www.dtic.mil/dtic/tr/fulltext/u2/a207997.pdf "7 March 1989." USAWC Military Studies Program paper; Student papers, ii, 34 p.; 28 cm.

D'Este, C., "Patton's Finest Hour," *The Quarterly Journal of Military History*, Spring (2001): 13-16. Retrieved from
http://library.norwich.edu/login?url=https://search-

proquest-com.library.norwich.edu/docview/223685754?accountid=12871.

Giarrusso, Joseph Martin, "Against all odds: the story of the 106th Infantry Division in the Battle of the Bulge" (1998). Master's Theses. 1743. DOI: https://doi.org/10.31979/etd.mhut-9n72 https://scholarworks.sjsu.edu/etd_theses/1743.

Gordon, Marvin F., "Physiography and Military Perception The Cases of Plan XVII, the Ardennes, Caporetto, and the Taebaek Split." *Army History*, no. 39 (1996): 18-27. www.jstor.org/stable/26304341.

Gurley, Franklin Louis, "Policy Versus Strategy: The Defense of Strasbourg in Winter 1944-1945." *The Journal of Military History* 58, no. 3 (1994): 481-514. doi:10.2307/2944136.

Hull, Mike, "Slog Through the Hurtgen Forest," *Military History*, January 2018, 36-39.

Middleton, Drew, "The Battle that Sealed Germany's Fate." *The New York Times*, December 16, 1984, sec. 6.

Mitchell, Ralph M., "The 101st Airborne Division's Defense of Bastogne." *Combat Studies Institute*, US Army Command & General Staff College, (1986).

Nash, Douglas, "KESTERNICH: The Battle That Saved the Bulge." *Army History*, no. 109 (2018): 34-51.

https://www-jstor-org.library.norwich.edu/stable/26493734.

Schwendemann, Heinrich, "Drastic Measures to Defend the Reich at the Oder and the Rhine…: A Forgotten Memorandum of Albert Speer of 18 Match 1945." *Journal of Contemporary History* Vol. 38, No. 4 (2003): 597-614.

Weinberg, Gerhard L., "German Plans for Victory, 1944-45.", *Central European History* 26, no. 2 (1993): 215-228.
http://www.jstor.org.library.norwich.edu/stable/4546332.

Yelton, David K., "Ein Volk Steht Auf": The German Volkssturm and Nazi Strategy, 1944-45." *The Journal of Military History* 64, no. 4 (2000): 1061-083. doi:10.2307/2677267.

Other

Caddick-Adams, Peter, "The Battle of the Bulge." (Power-Point presentation, Dan Hill's History from Home, March 25, 2020)
https://www.danhillmilitaryhistorian.com/archive

About the Author

Jason Boswell currently serves as in the United States military. He enjoys spending time with his family whenever possible. Jason grew up as a military child and got to experience different cultures all over the world. After High School, he attended Utah State University, where he married his high school sweetheart. After gaining an appreciation for history, he continued his education at Norwich University, where his studies concluded into his published work.

Printed in Great Britain
by Amazon